# FAMOUS FLYING MACHINES

## A Quick History of Flight with 7 Authentic Models to Make and Fly

by Leon Baxter

Ideals Children's Books • Nashville, Tennessee

# Contents




Published by Ideals Publishing Corporation
Nashville, Tennessee 37210
Printed and bound in the U.S.A.

Created and designed by Treld Bicknell.

ISBN 0-8249-8532-X

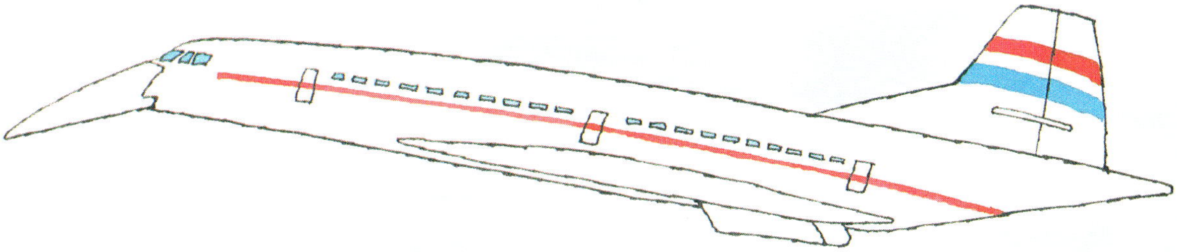

# Introduction

This book is a short history of aviation told through the stories of some of the world's most important and fascinating flying machines.

From the Wright Flyer to the space shuttle, aircraft have developed—through war and peace—from a simple powered glider to a rocket-propelled craft that is at home in outer space. Seven of the most popular airplanes are included here, in authentic detail, for you to cut out, assemble, and fly.

By following the step-by-step instructions, you will be able to make your own Blériot monoplane for crossing the English Channel, a Spitfire and a Messerschmitt to meet in exciting aerial combat, or an elegant, supersonic Concorde to take you to the other side of the world faster than the speed of sound.

You will be in control—overseeing production, checking the trim, and selecting the best flying conditions for your models. Using the basic body, wing, and tail shapes shown here, you can go on to design and build your own planes for the future. Join the Wright brothers, Louis Blériot, and the aircraft designers of Boeing and NASA as one of the pioneers of flight.

*Leon Baxter*

# Construction

## Materials

scissors

hobby knife

paper paste or quick-drying glue

paper fasteners

modeling clay or cork

thumbtacks

paper clips

buttons

double-sided adhesive tape

## Construction

All of the aircraft in this book are constructed in the same way.

Before you begin, study the pictures of the model that you want to make.

Remove the model pages from the book by carefully cutting along the dotted lines printed at the inner edge of each model page. When the pages are free, you can assemble each model by following the same steps.

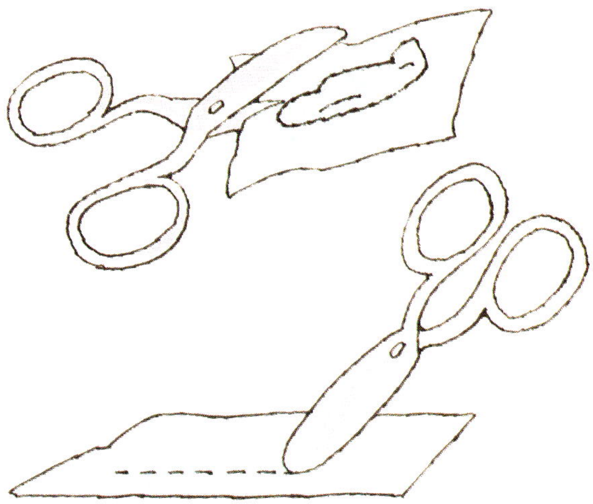

1. Carefully cut out the model parts along the solid black lines.

2. Score and fold along the dotted lines. To score, use the tip of closed scissors to make a light groove along each dotted line—this creates a neater fold.

3. Follow the numbered sequence of diagrams on the model pages to assemble the models in the correct order.

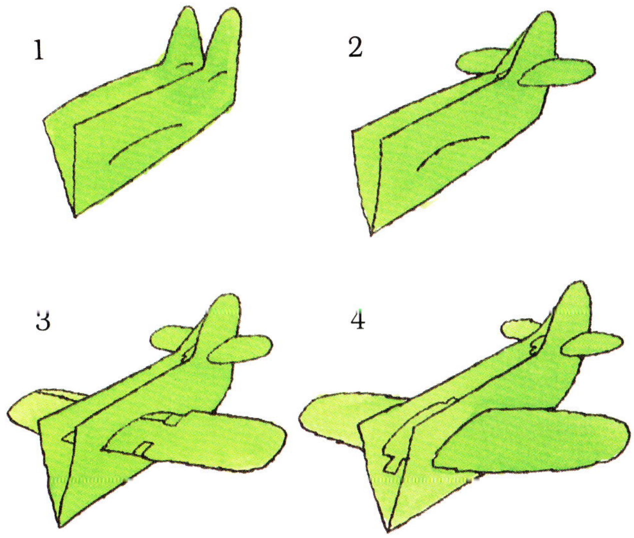


4. Ask an adult to help you to cut along the solid curved lines with a hobby knife.
5. Fold the wings and insert them into the curved wing slot; then unfold them to secure.

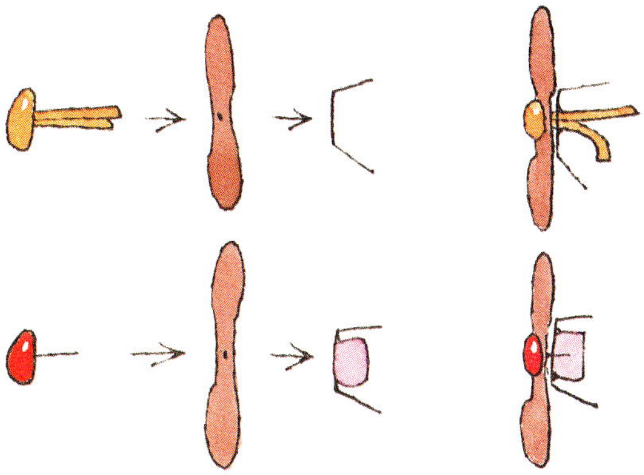

6. To attach a propeller which does not spin, use a paper fastener. Push the fastener through the center of the propeller and into the aircraft's nose; fold back the ends.

   To attach a propeller which spins, push a thumbtack through the propeller and the nose of the plane into a small piece of modeling clay or cork inside the nose. Don't make it too tight or the propeller will not spin.

Start with this much—add more if needed.

NOTE: Do not use too much clay or cork because its weight can keep the plane from flying properly.

7. Use buttons for wheels. Since they don't need to roll, use glue or double-sided tape to attach buttons to the wheel struts. Glue the paper wheels to the buttons. *Do not* use a button tail wheel; your aircraft needs to be heavier at the front.

# Trimming and Flying

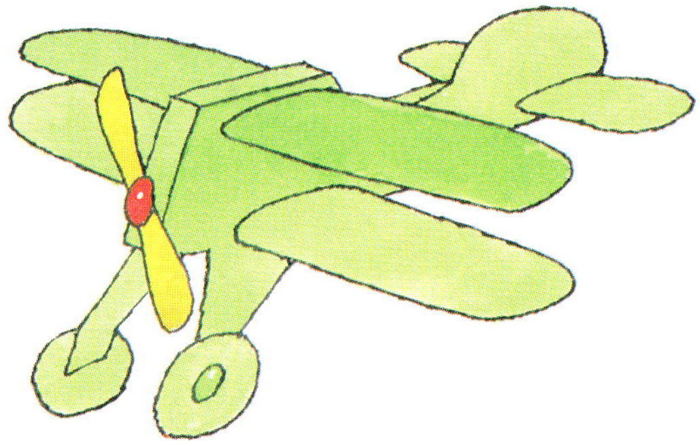

These little models are lightweight and fly best indoors. Large rooms and long hallways make good flying spaces.

If you are flying your plane outdoors, choose a sunny day when the wind is still.

Puddles and wet grass quickly destroy paper models.

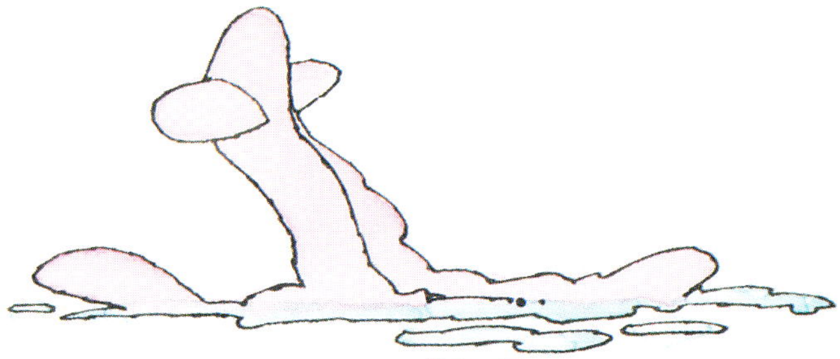

## Trimming

Trimming your aircraft means putting it into good order and, especially with models, arranging it so that the balance is just right for a successful flight.

Pilots of aircraft, large or small, follow a list of trim procedures before take-off.

## Testing

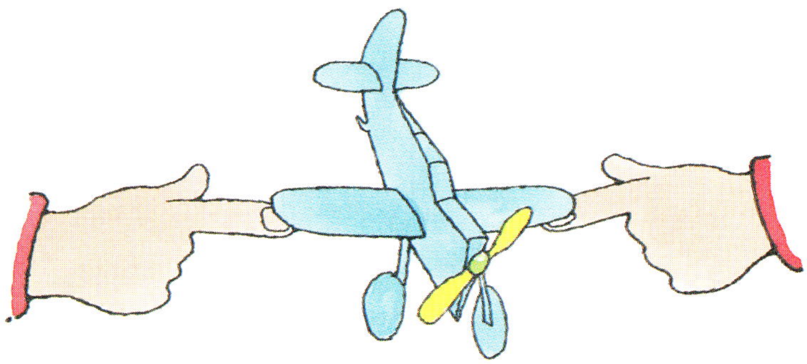

1. Your aircraft should be heavier at the nose. Test this by gently lifting the plane by the wing tips—it should tip forward. Add more weight, if necessary, using modeling clay, cork, or paper clips.

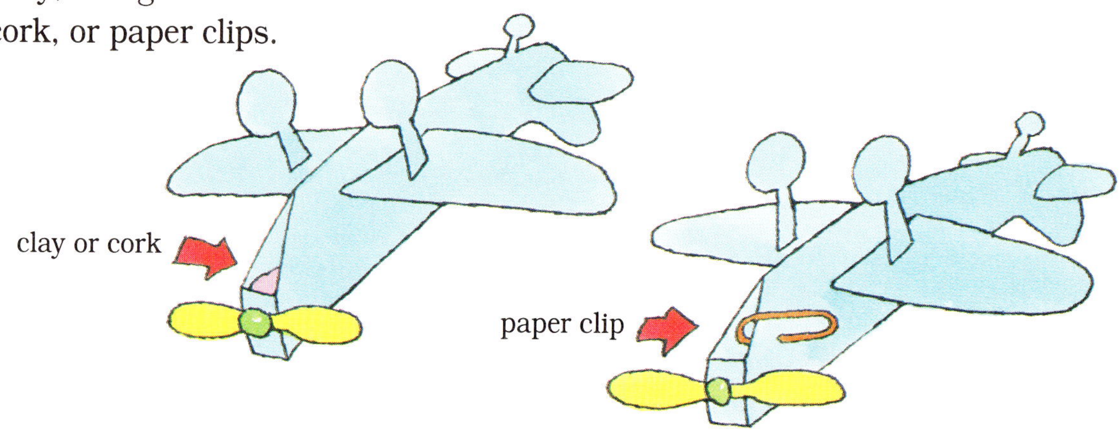

2. The tail fin should be straight and the tail flaps slightly up.
3. Wheel struts need to point straight down with landing wheels level.

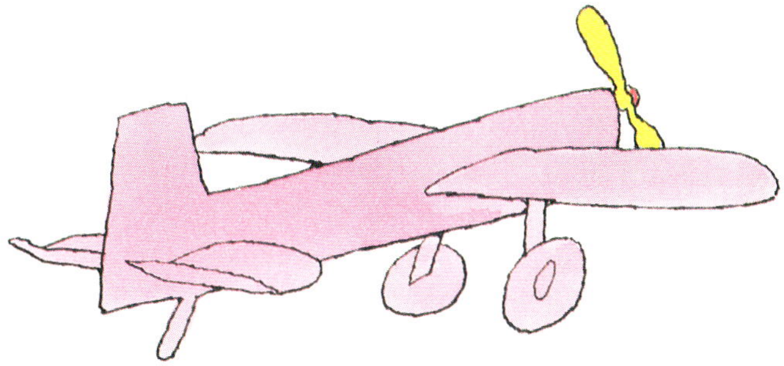

## Flying

When the model is ready for take-off, launch it gently and smoothly with the nose pointing slightly **down.** If launched with the nose up, it will stall.

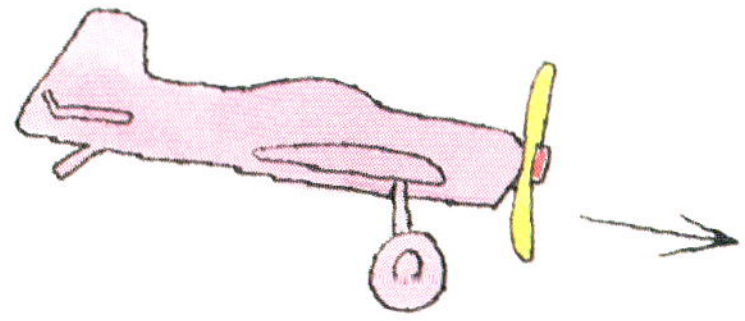

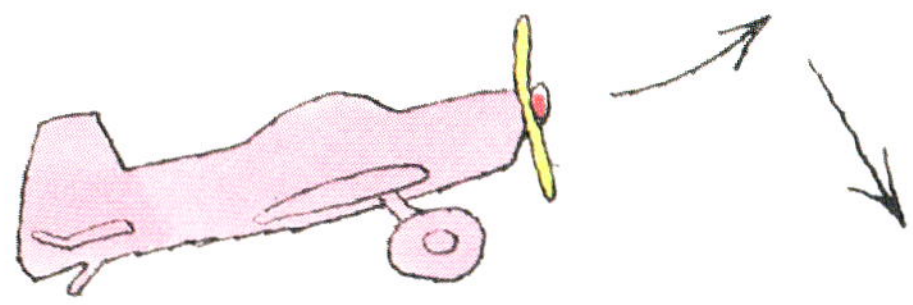

The plane should fly in a smooth glide. If it flutters and falls to the ground, the nose is too light—add a little more weight.

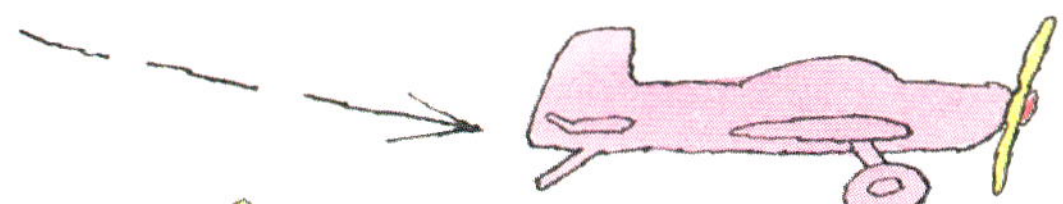

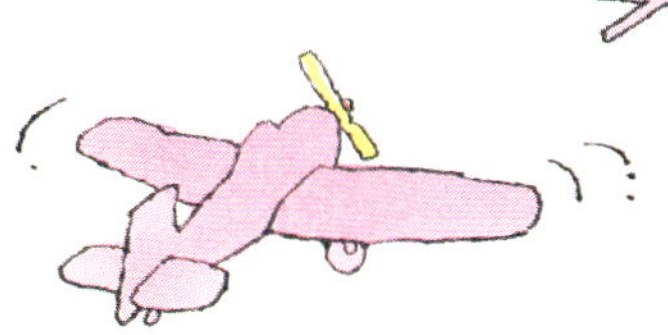

If it stalls, bend the flaps **down** slightly.

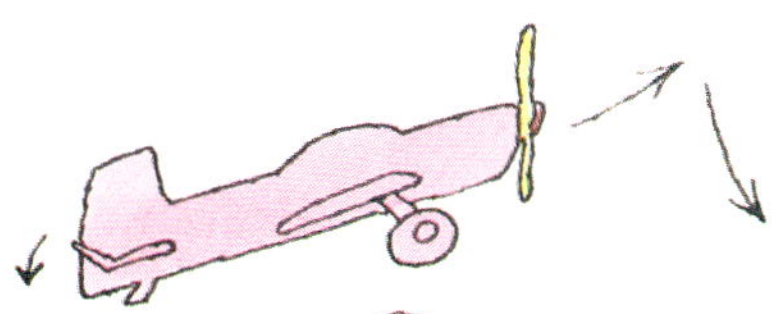

If it dives, bend the flaps **up** slightly.

With button wheels, your plane should fly smoothly and land neatly. Careful trimming and practice will make you an expert pilot.

Happy flying!

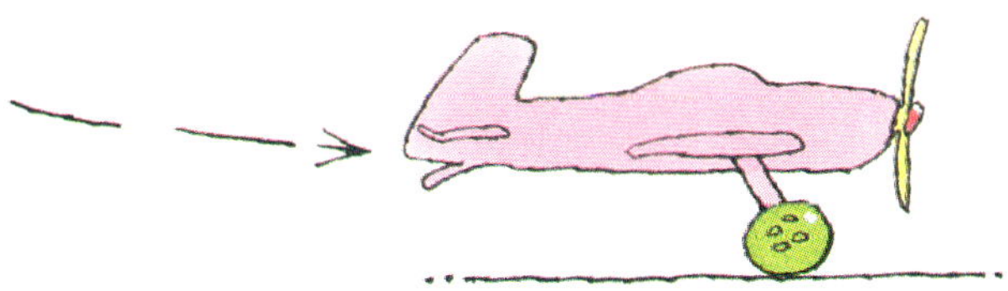

# The Wright Brothers

The Wright brothers were the first to build and successfully fly a motor-powered aircraft. They called their planes the Flyers.

Since ancient times, people have sought a way to imitate birds and soar through the air. Throughout the ages, they tried many methods—man-made wings in ancient Greece, man-carrying kites in 13th-century China, and early hang-gliders in Renaissance Italy. Nothing worked until the 18th century when Frenchmen Joseph and Etienne Montgolfier launched their huge, hot-air balloons. Thus began the age of air travel for sporting as well as practical purposes. Balloons and, later, airships, were used in war and peace.

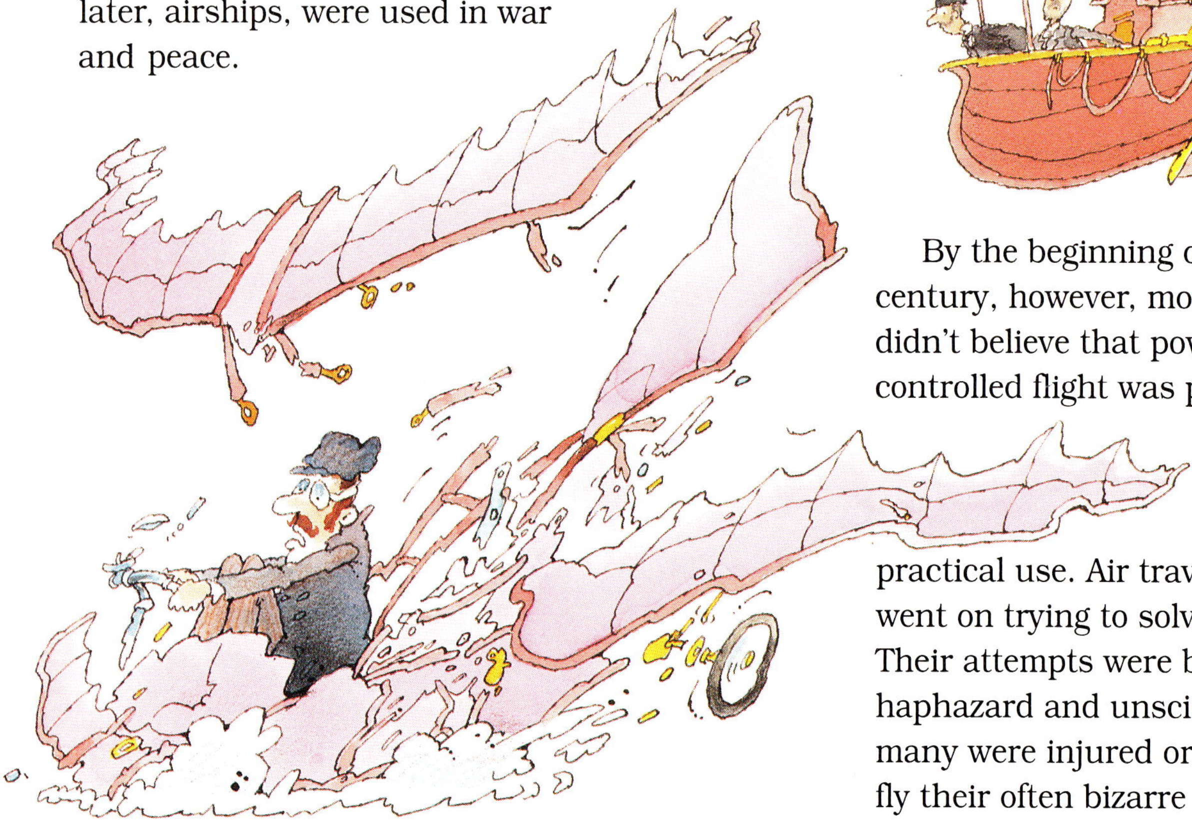

By the beginning of the 20th century, however, most people still didn't believe that powered, pilot-controlled flight was possible for practical use. Air travel enthusiasts went on trying to solve the problem. Their attempts were brave but often haphazard and unscientific, and many were injured or killed trying to fly their often bizarre aircraft.

In the United States lived two young engineers, Wilbur and Orville Wright, who designed, made, repaired, and sold bicycles from their workshop in Dayton, Ohio. They became interested in making and flying an airplane in the very late years of the 19th century. They applied to this task their skills as engineers and inventors, as well as the same careful, logical methods of testing that they applied to their bicycles.

The Wrights began by making big kites and gliders which used air currents to stay aloft, as birds do. For four years they carefully studied the "how" and "why" of flight, trying to learn about control and stability in the air.

The Wright brothers' observations helped them build better and better gliders. They made several test flights and became experienced pilots.

At last, the Wright Brothers designed and built a small engine and fitted it to a double-winged glider. On Thursday, December 17, 1903, Orville Wright made the first engine-powered, pilot-controlled flight in an airplane at Kitty Hawk, North Carolina. This historic flight lasted just 12 seconds.

The two brothers did not hurry to tell the world what they had done. Very few people took notice of their successful flight, and the Wrights still sold more bicycles than airplanes. For two more years they worked privately—until October, 1905, when Wilbur made a 25-mile flight in their new plane, the Wright Flyer III.

Still the world ignored the Wright brothers and their airplanes, and so they stopped flying for a few years. Meanwhile the French—those fearless balloonists—began building airplanes and making test flights.

The Wright brothers returned to the air in 1908 and proved that they were still the best. With a 77-mile flight lasting more than two hours, Wilbur Wright won the Michelin prize and established an official world flight record.

Cut along this dotted line to remove page.

# Wright Flyer model

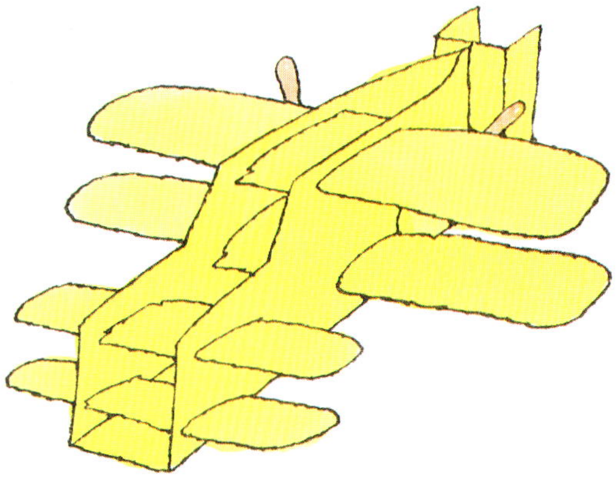

Cut along the solid lines.

Fold along the dotted lines.

fuselage—interior

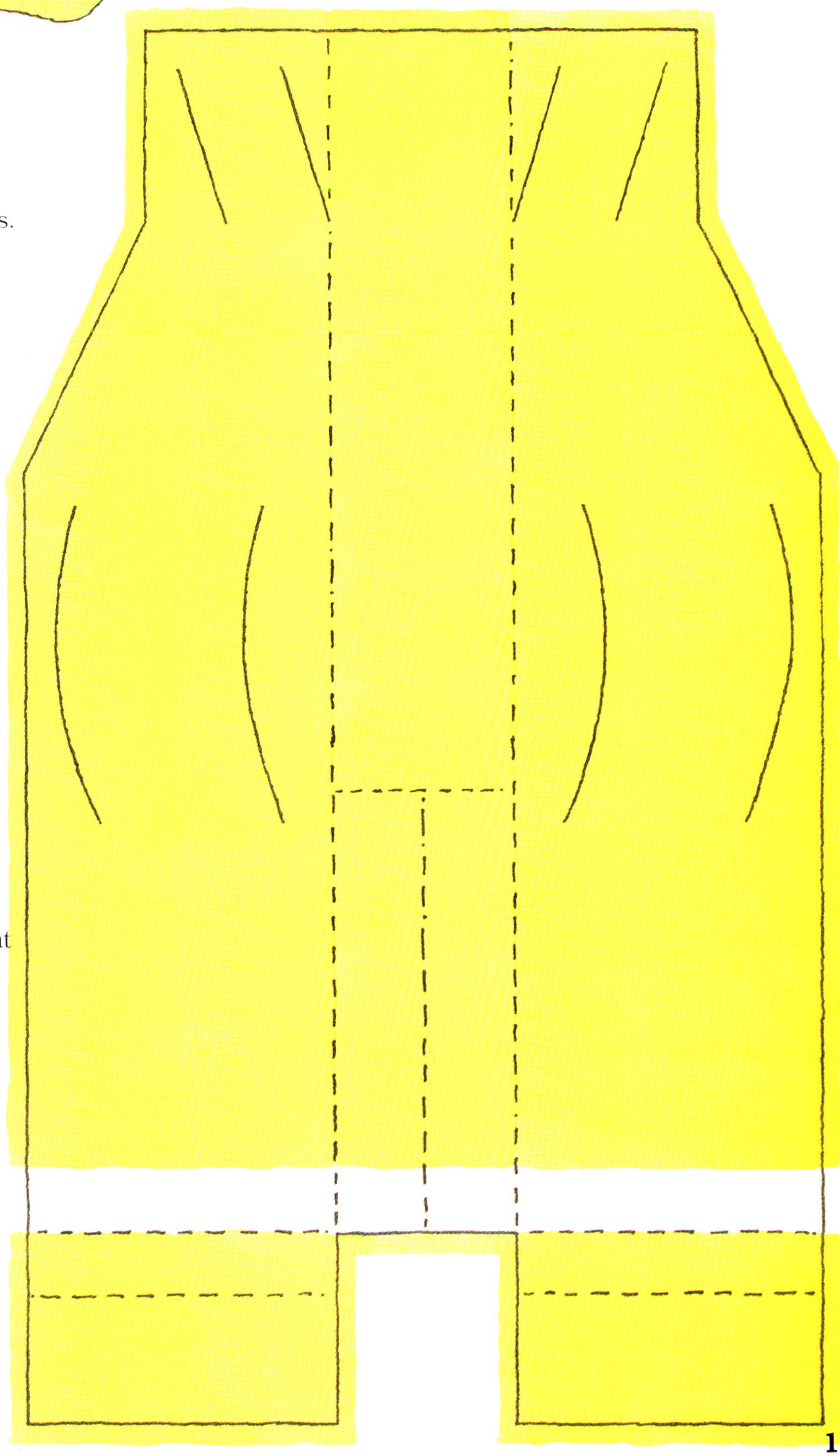

Orville Wright's first flight

Time—10:35 A.M.
Date—December 17, 1903
Location—Kitty Hawk, North Carolina
Distance—120 feet
Duration—12 seconds

Wilbur Wright's world record flight

Date—December 31, 1908
Location—Auvours, France
Distance—77 miles
Duration—2 hours, 20 minutes, 23 seconds

## The Wright Flyer—assembly

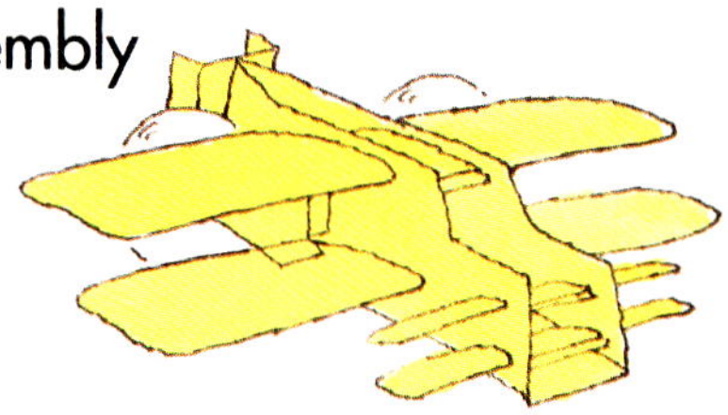

Cut along the solid lines.

Fold along the dotted lines.

fuselage—exterior

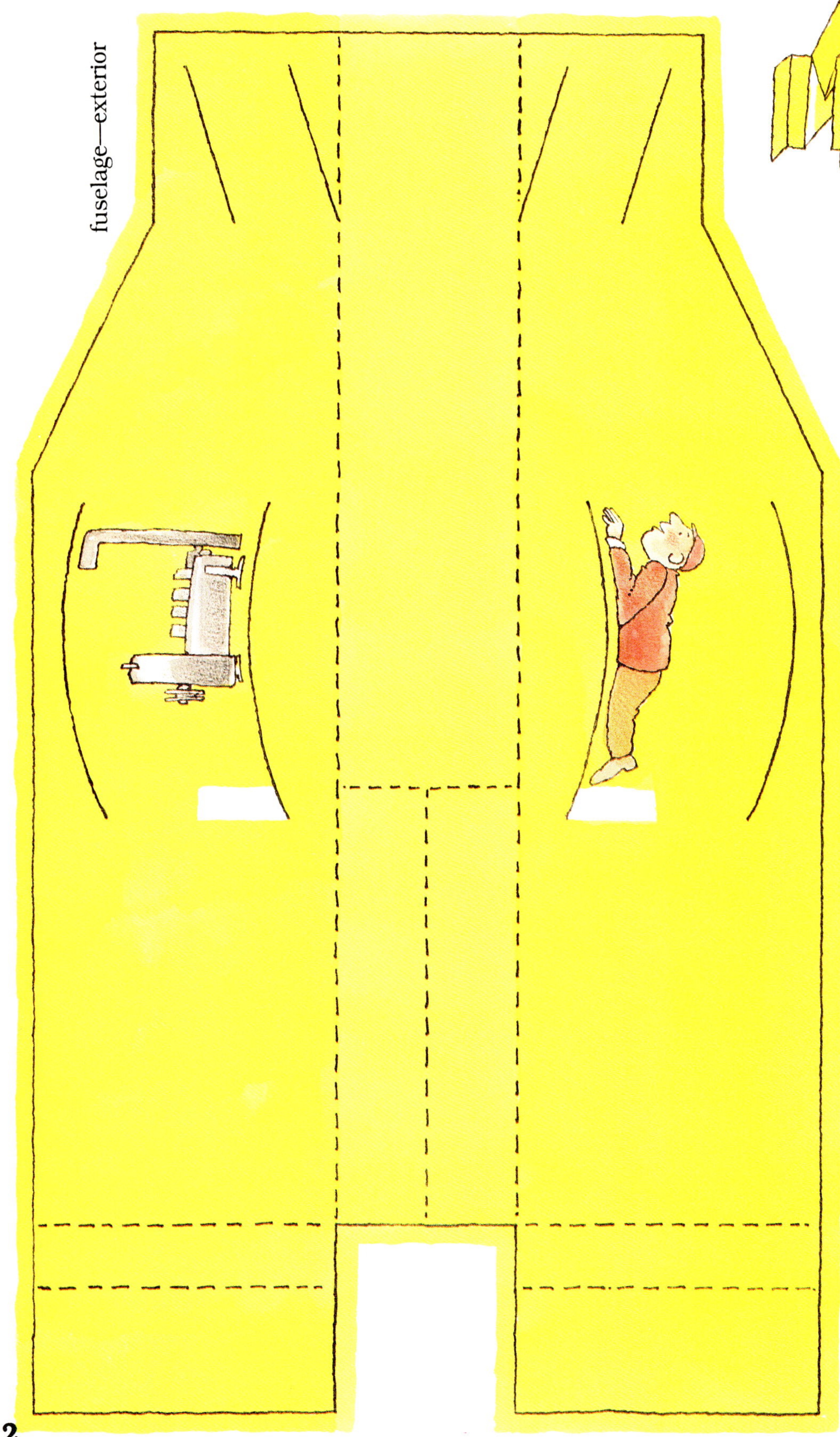

1. Score, fold, and glue the fuselage (body of plane).

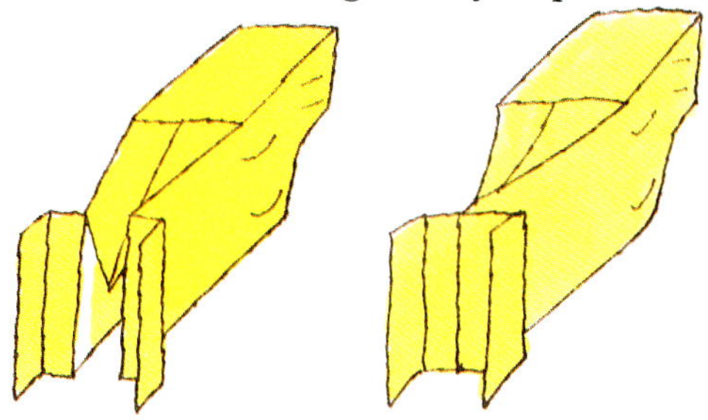

2. Carefully cut the curved wing slots and insert the main wings.

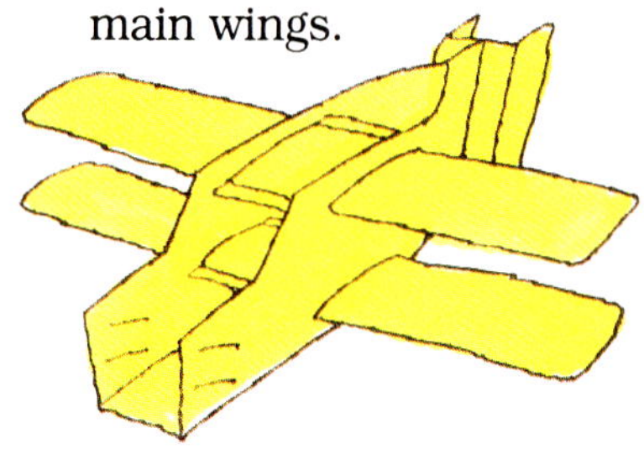

3. Carefully cut the nose wing slots and insert the nose wings.

4. Score, fold, and glue the propeller chains to the fuselage and wings.

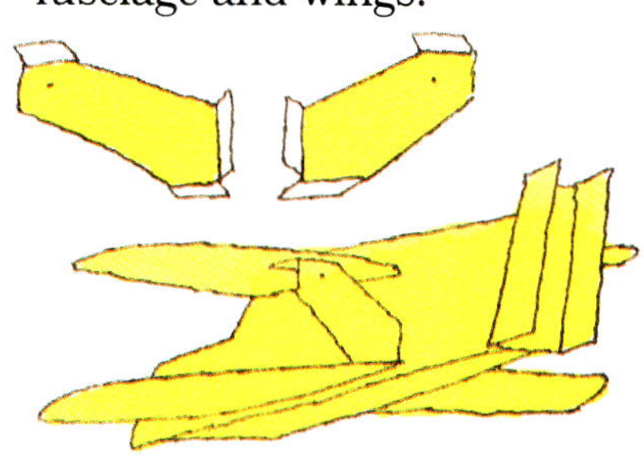

5. Mount propellers at the back.

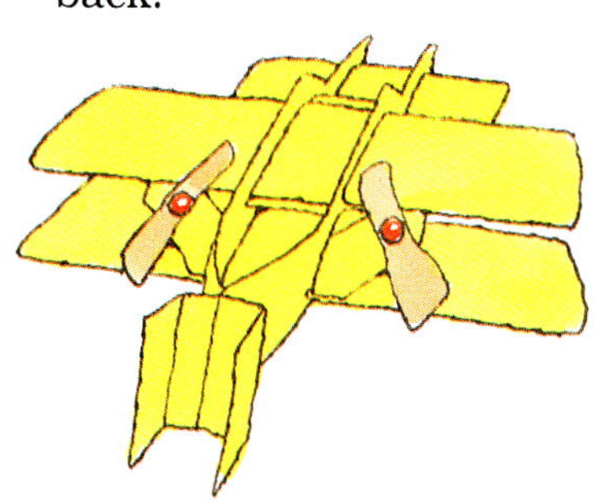

Cut along this dotted line to remove page.

Cut along this dotted line to remove page.

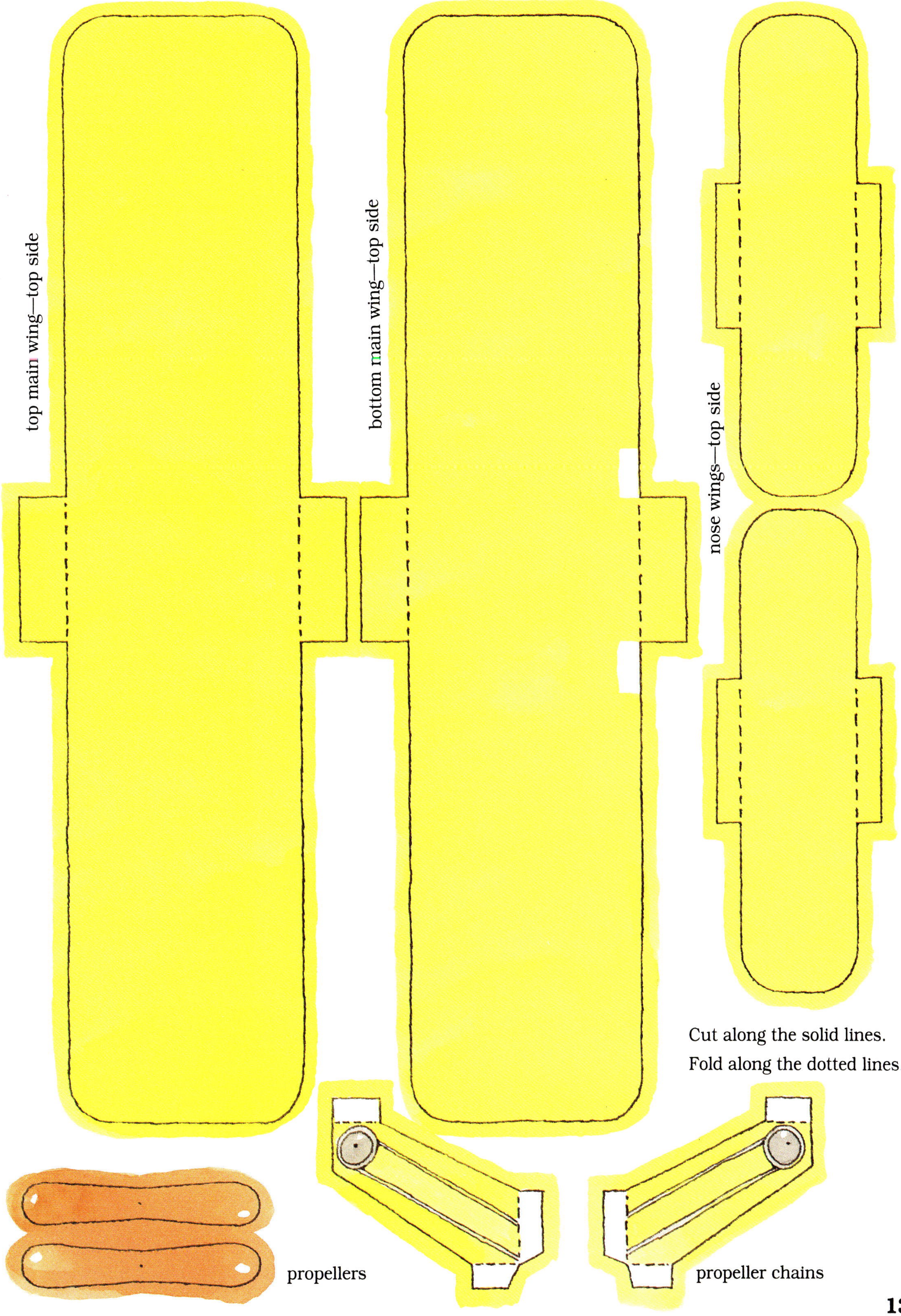


Cut along the solid lines.
Fold along the dotted lines.

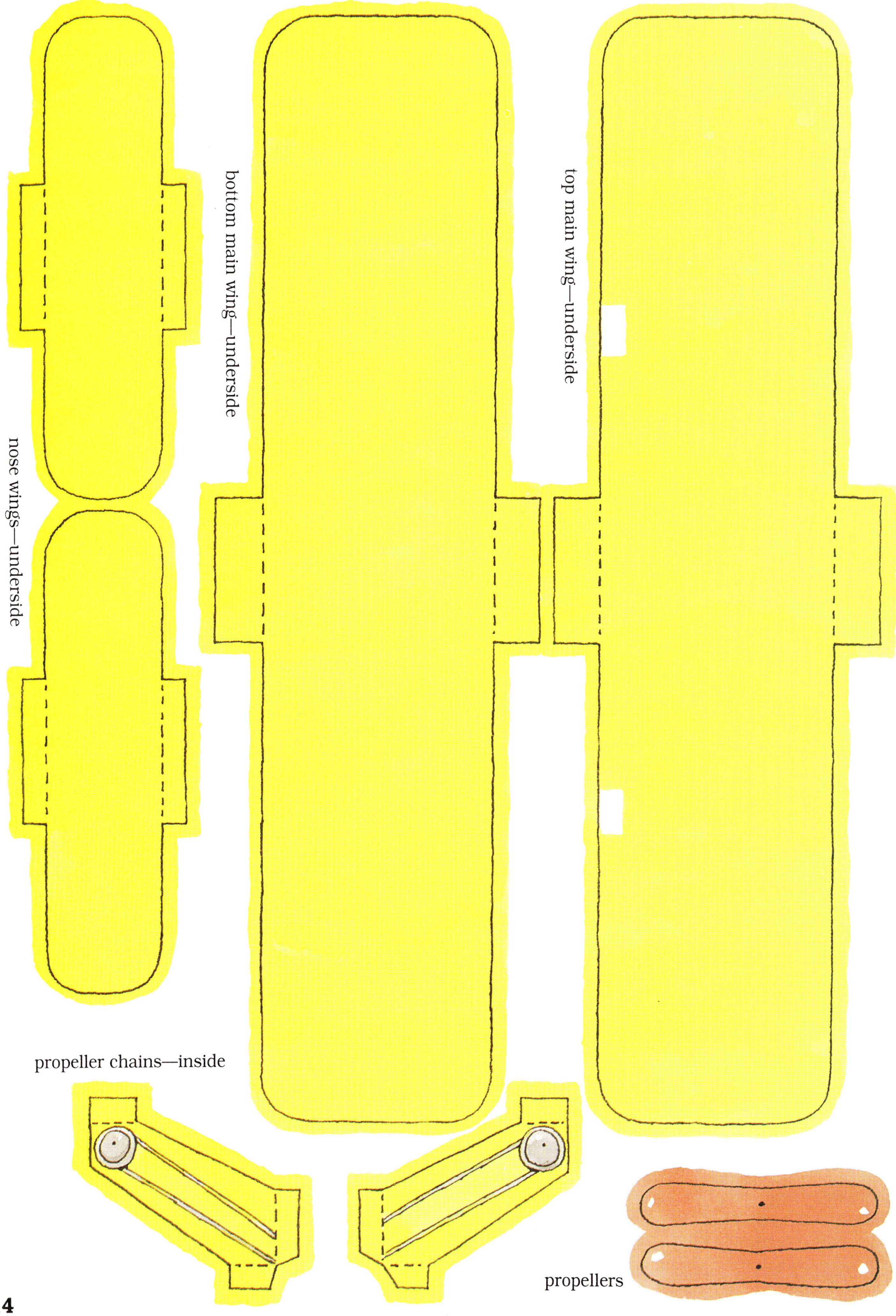


Cut along this dotted line to remove page.

# Blériot Flies the Channel

Louis Blériot became the first person to fly across the English Channel, the 21-mile stretch of water separating England from France.

Louis Blériot was a French engineer who had made his fortune selling spare automobile parts. He wasn't a great designer or a very good pilot, but he was brave and enthusiastic. His early attempts to fly often ended in failure—he was an unlikely trailblazer.

While many people still doubted whether airplanes had any practical use, an increasing number of sporting flyers took to the sky in search of fame—and fortune! In 1909, the owner of the London *Daily Mail* newspaper offered a £1000 prize (then worth about $5000) to the first person to fly across the English Channel.

In July of that year, three men took up the challenge. They waited near Calais, on the west coast of France, for good flying weather. Englishman Hubert Latham made the first attempt in his Levasseur Antoinette IV, but he fell into the sea after only eight miles.

A Russian aristocrat, Count Charles de Lambert made the second attempt in one of his two Wright Flyers. But having the best aircraft did not help Count de Lambert. He eventually crashed both of his planes and gave up in disgust.

Louis Blériot was nobody's favorite to win the prize. He had spent his entire fortune on his passion for flying and had to borrow money to make this attempt to fly the Channel. His plane, the Blériot XI, was a fragile contraption of canvas and wood, and it held a small, under-powered engine. Blériot himself was on crutches!

Early on Sunday, July 25, 1909, with favorable weather conditions, Louis Blériot put his crutches into the back of his plane and took off at 4:41 A.M. to fly west toward the misty coast of England. With no instruments to measure speed, height, or direction, he headed over the sea. As the coast of France slipped out of sight, he followed the route of ships below, which he hoped were sailing toward Dover.

At 5:17 A.M., Blériot cleared the high, white cliffs of Dover and crash-landed in a field a few miles inland. His prize-winning journey of almost 24 miles had taken him just 36 minutes.

There were great celebrations in London and Paris, and many people offered to buy Blériot monoplanes. After all his years of dedication, Blériot became rich and famous. And more importantly, the world at last began to take flying seriously.

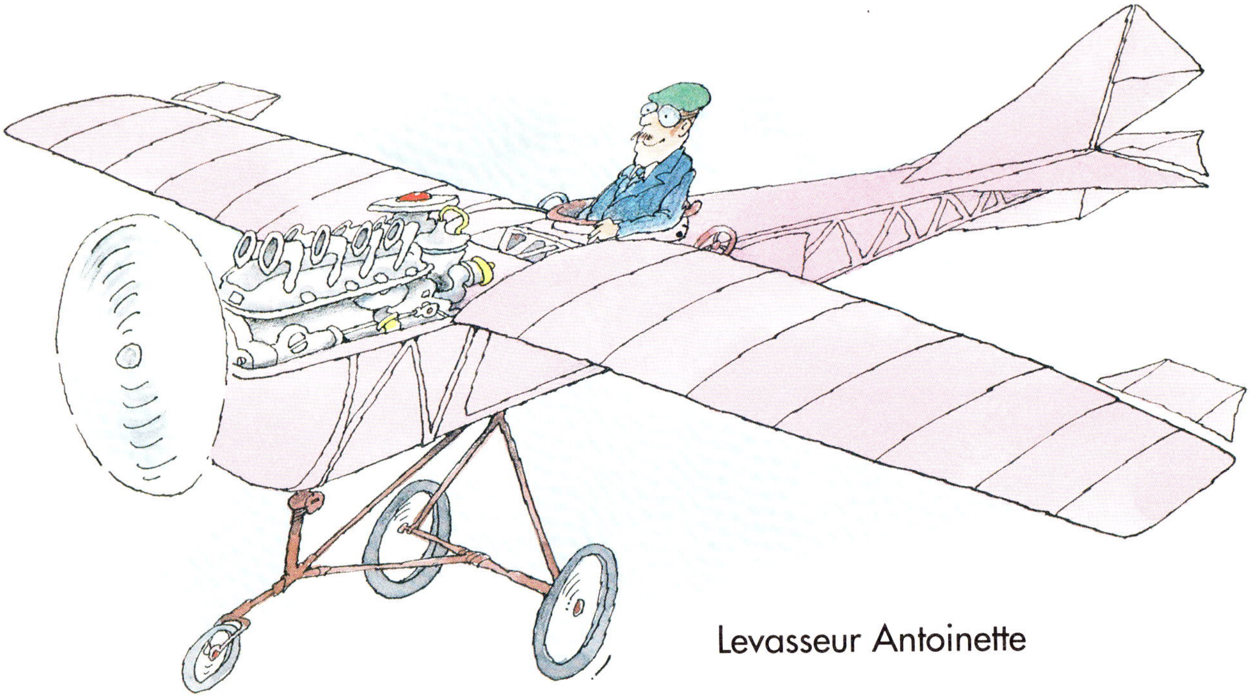

Levasseur Antoinette

From the beginning, flying fever gripped the French; and in the early 1900s, there were more Frenchmen in the air than any other nationality.

Léon Levasseur was a French engineer who designed not only aircraft but also the engines to power them. Among his most successful engines was the Antoinette design, and between 1903 and 1909, the Antoinette powered many of the most airworthy craft.

Alberto Santos-Dumont was a Brazilian flying enthusiast who came to live in France. Already an experienced balloonist, Santos-Dumont flew 772 feet in his unusual airplane, the *14 bis*, winning the 1906 Aero-Club of France prize for the first sustained flight in Europe. The *14 bis* was powered by one of Levasseur's Antoinette engines.

Santos-Dumont 14 bis

Cut along this dotted line to remove page.

# Blériot XI model

tail wing—underside

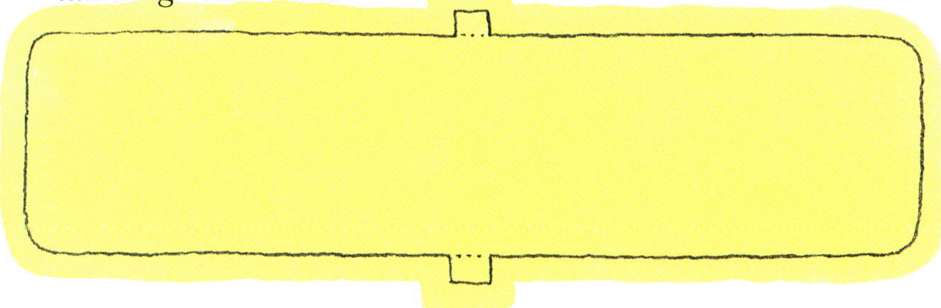

fuselage—interior

Cut along the solid lines.

Fold along the dotted lines.

## Blériot XI—assembly

fuselage—exterior

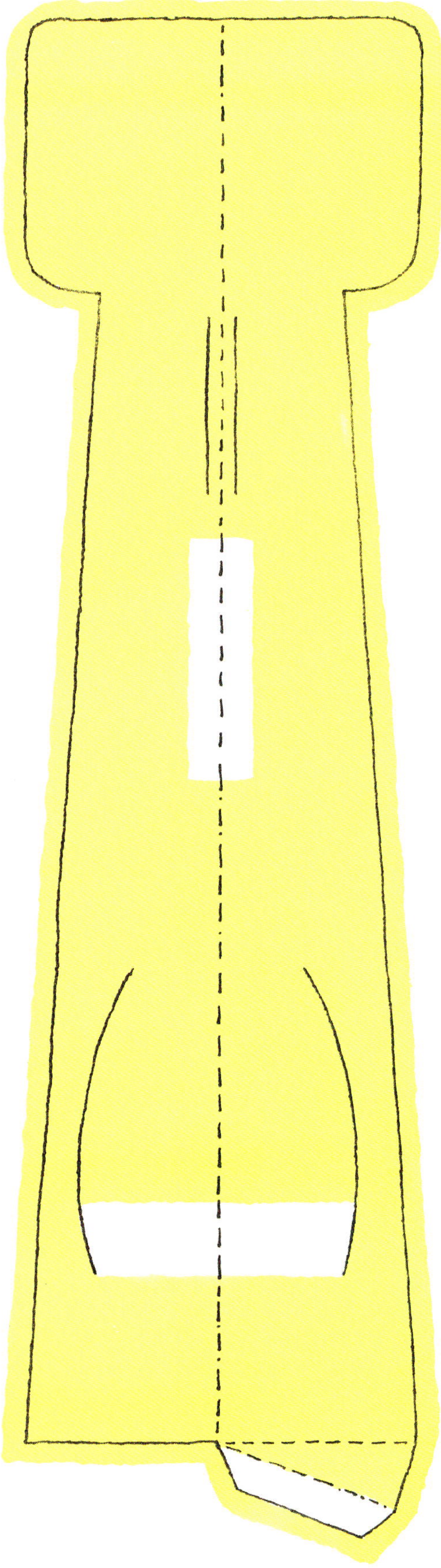

tail wing—top side

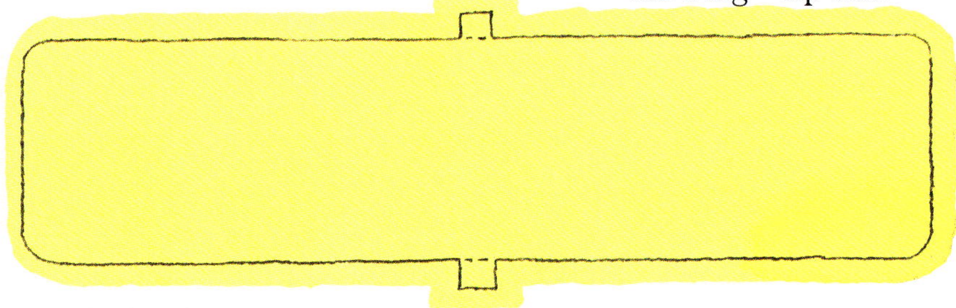

1. Fold fuselage, cut tail wing slot, and insert tail wing.

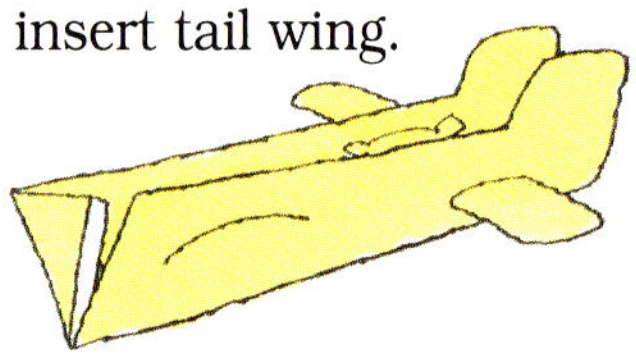

2. Glue sides of tail together.

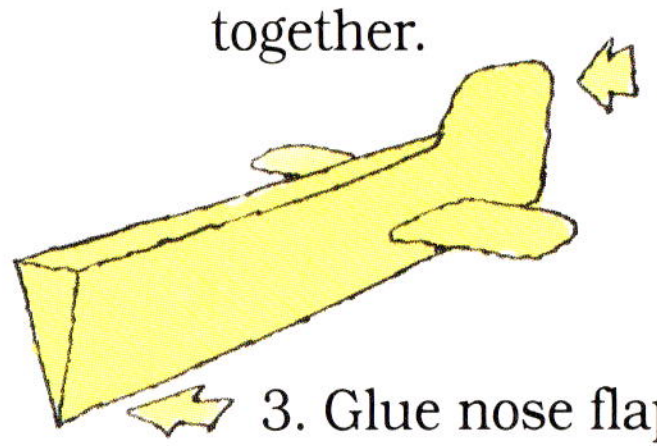

3. Glue nose flap to inside of body.

4. Carefully cut curved wing slot and insert main wing.

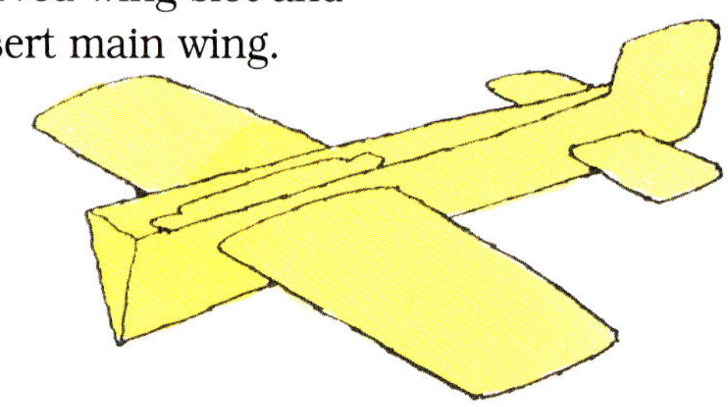

5. Fold and glue the undercarriage, as shown.

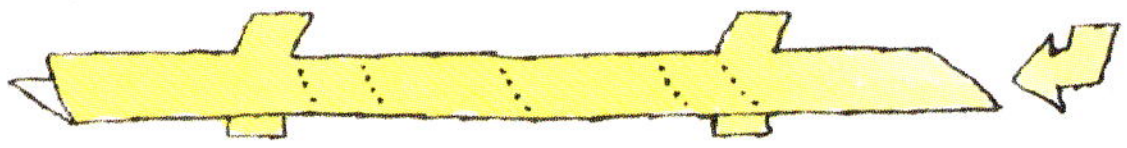

Then fold and glue the undercarriage to the fuselage.

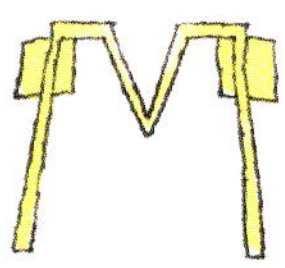

6. Glue wheels to the undercarriage, and fold and glue the tail wheel to the fuselage.

Cut along this dotted line to remove page.

Cut along this dotted line to remove page.

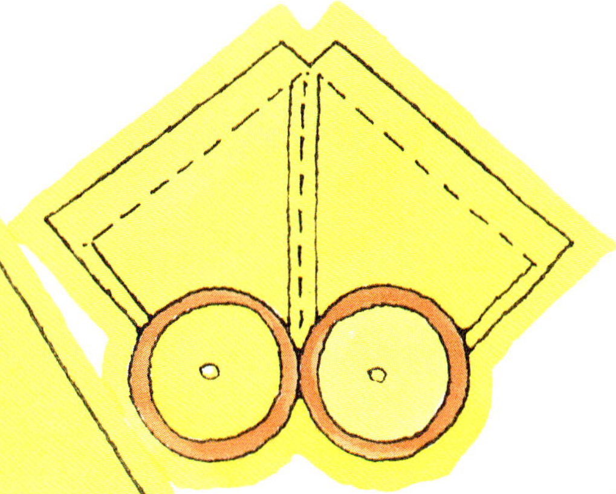


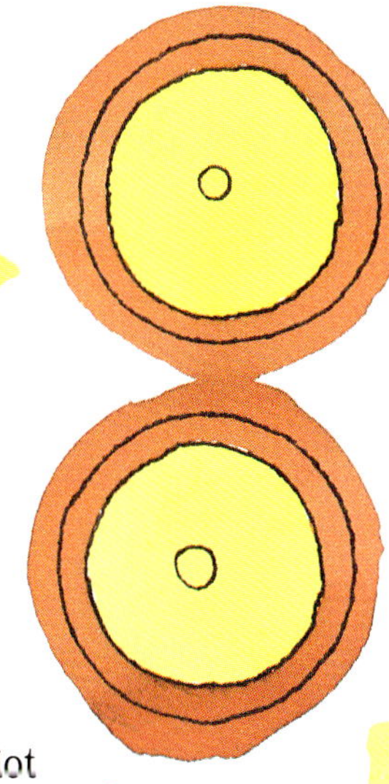


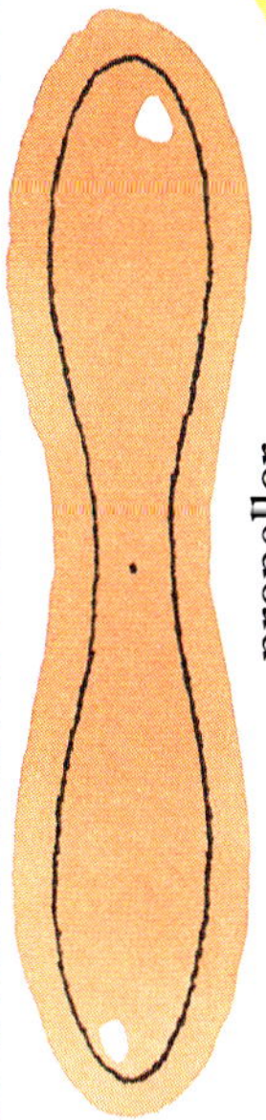

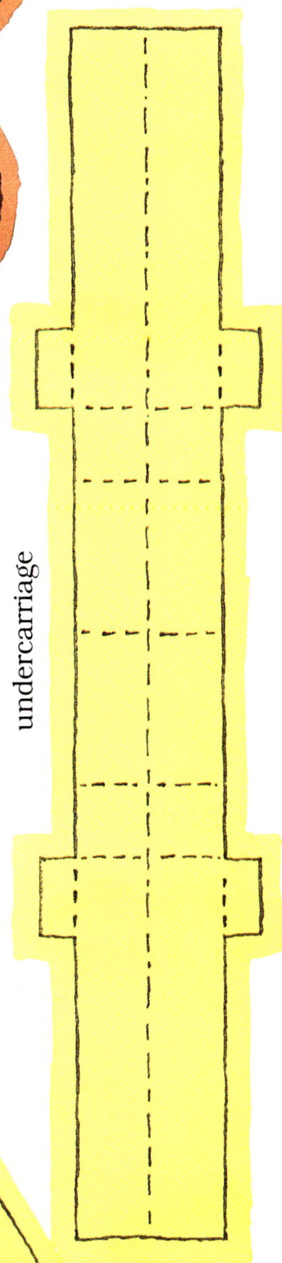


Cut along the solid lines.
Fold along the dotted lines.

7. Attach the propeller.

8. Fold Blériot and glue him into place.

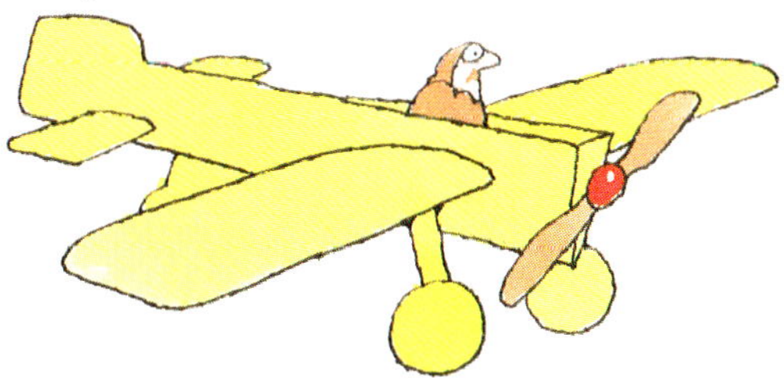

main wing—top side

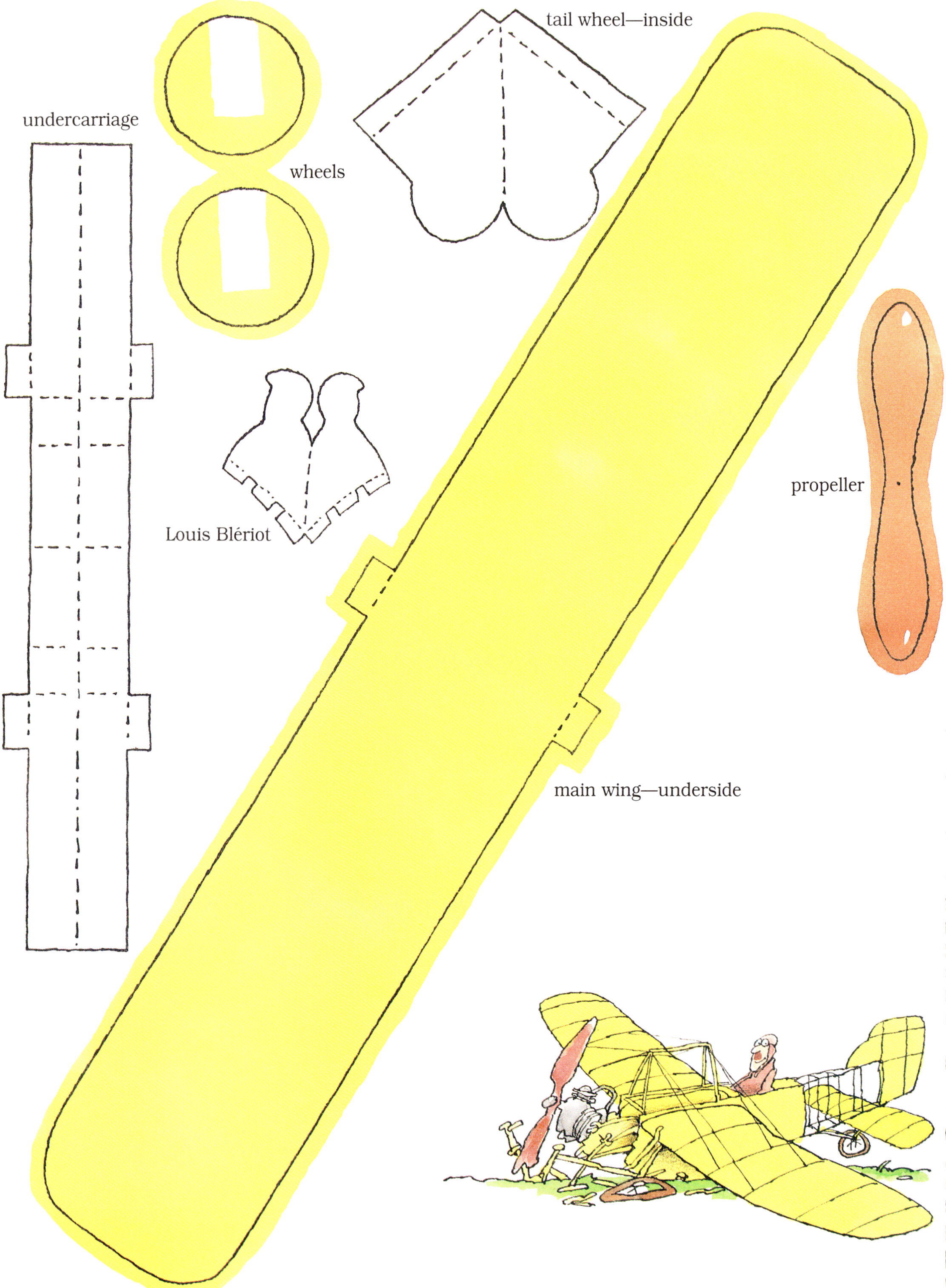

undercarriage

wheels

tail wheel—inside

Louis Blériot

propeller

main wing—underside

Cut along this dotted line to remove page.

# The Sopwith Camel

World War I was the first war in which airplanes were used as part of the fighting forces. Between 1914 and 1918, designers and engineers worked around the clock to produce stronger, faster, and more reliable planes.

At the beginning of the war, planes weren't equipped with guns or bombs but were used only as scouts. Pilots watched the enemy from the air, took photographs, and made maps to help the movement of tanks and troops on the ground.

Soon, because of their speed and agility, airplanes were used as fighters and fitted with guns and bombs for attack and defense. Pilots battled their rivals in the air—twisting, diving, and looping as they avoided enemy gunfire. The French won the first air combat victory on October 5, 1914.

One of the best of these new fighter planes was the Sopwith Camel, named after the great British flyer, T.O.M. Sopwith. It had a big engine and two large guns and could twist, dive, and loop with ease. The Camel had one major fault—it was so agile that only a very skilled pilot could control it. Poor handling caused it to go into a spin and crash.

Nevertheless, the speedy Camel was a favorite with pilots and became the most successful fighter plane of World War I, with 1,294 victories over enemy aircraft.

# Sopwith Camel model

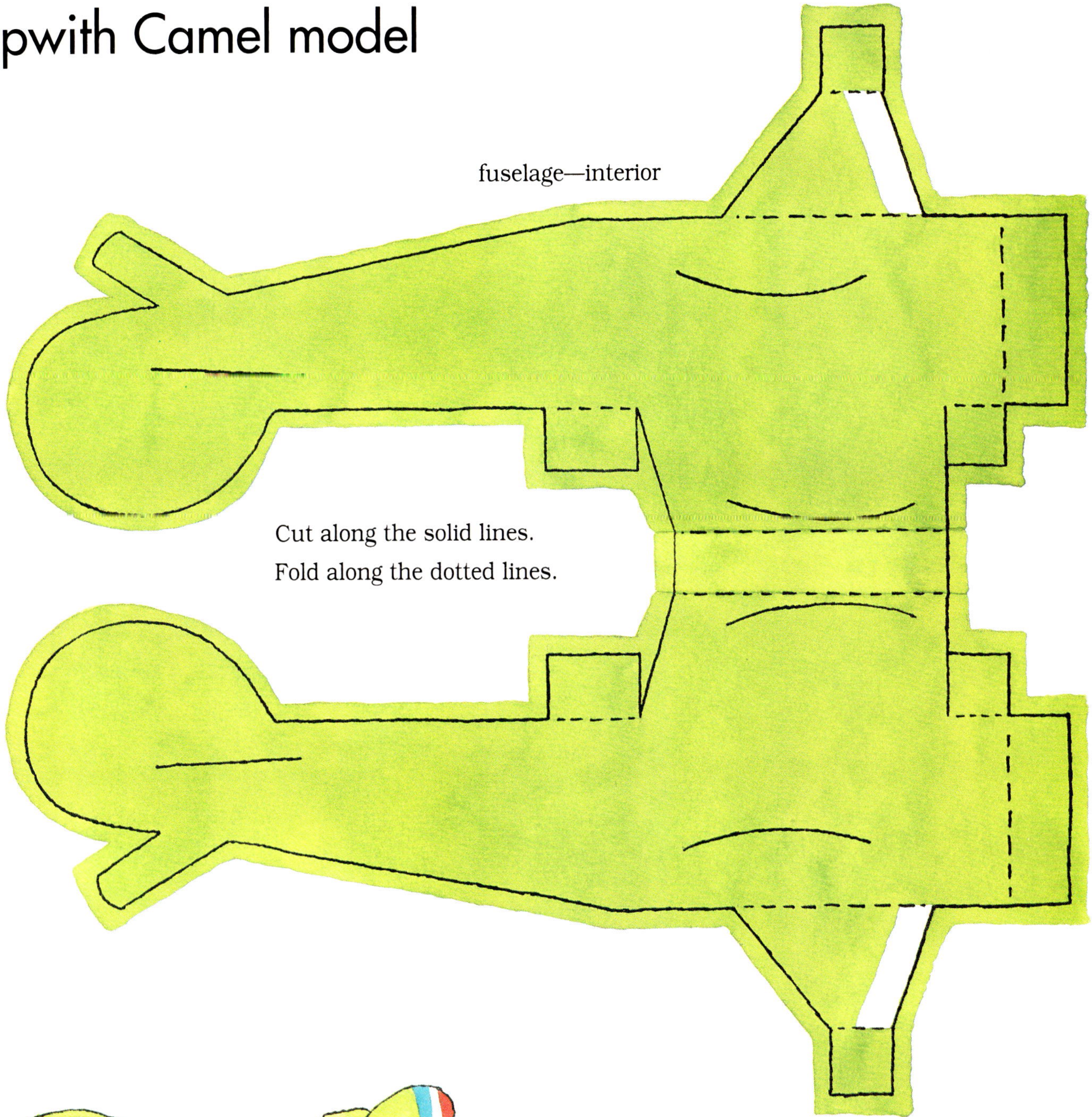


Cut along the solid lines.
Fold along the dotted lines.

tail wing—underside

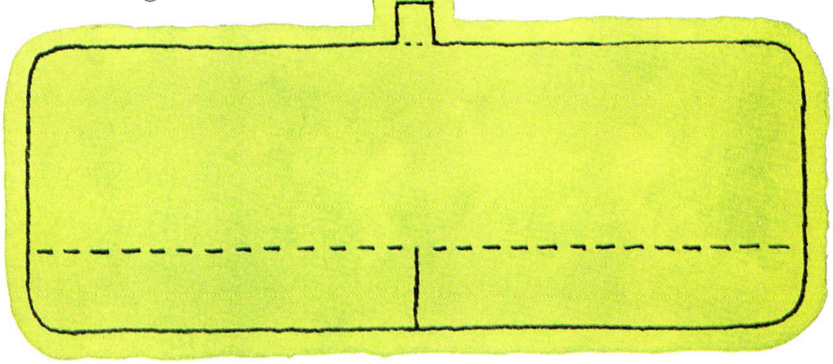

Cut along this dotted line to remove page.

# Sopwith Camel—assembly

Cut along the solid lines.

Fold along the dotted lines.

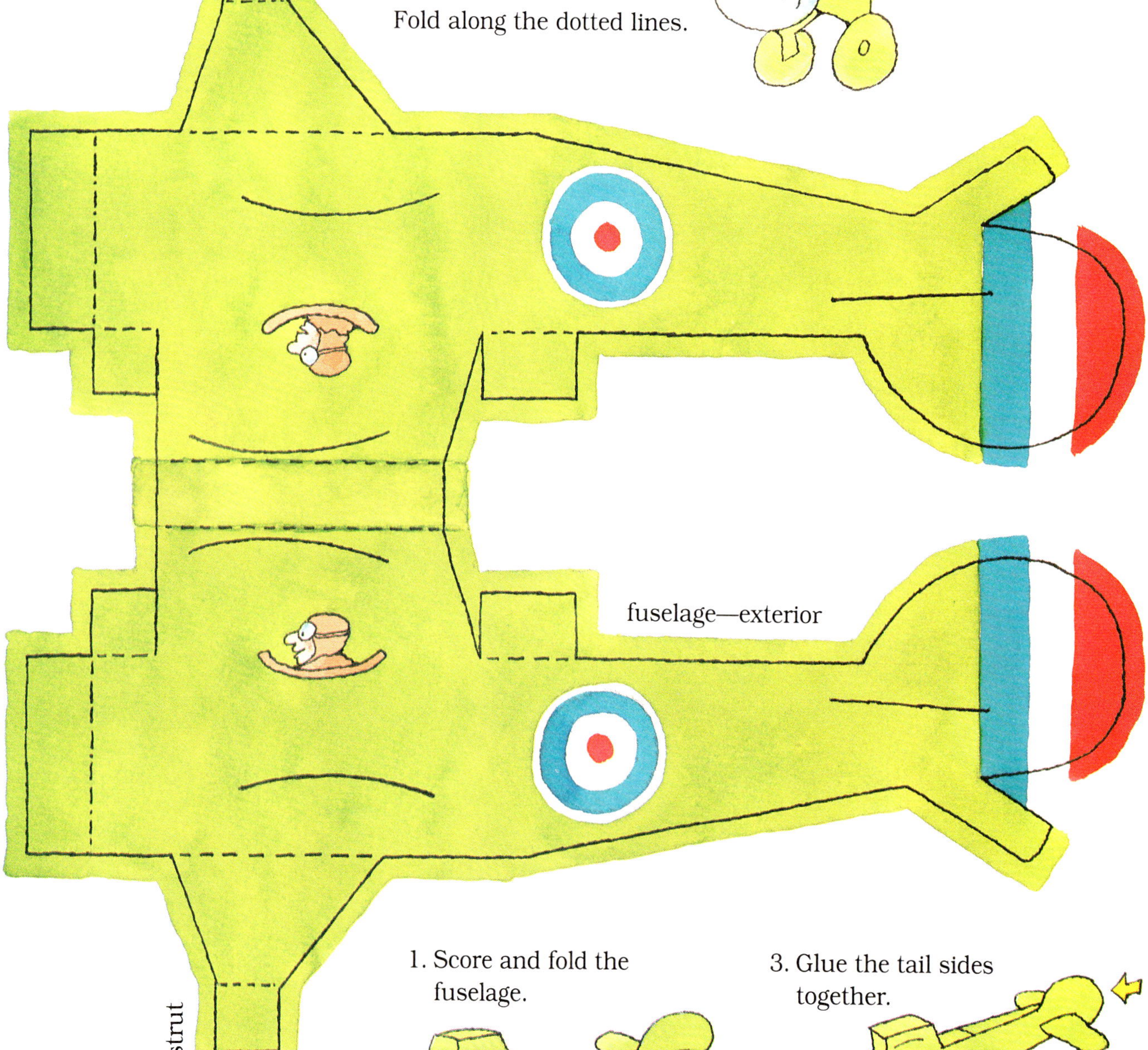


1. Score and fold the fuselage.

2. Cut a wing slot and insert tail wing.

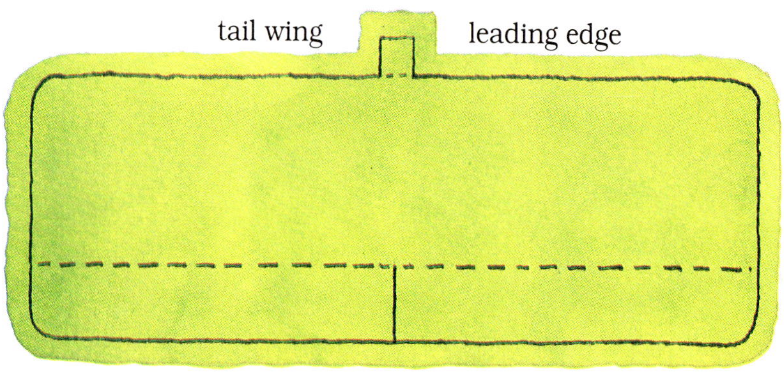


3. Glue the tail sides together.

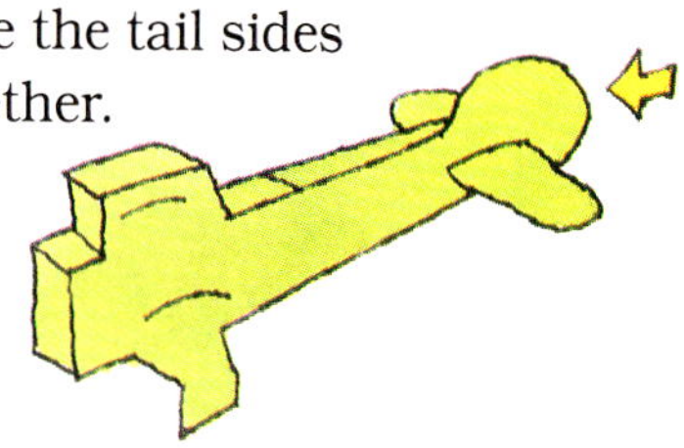

4. Cut the wing slots and insert the main wings.

5. Glue the fuselage together.

Cut along this dotted line to remove page.

Cut along this dotted line to remove page.

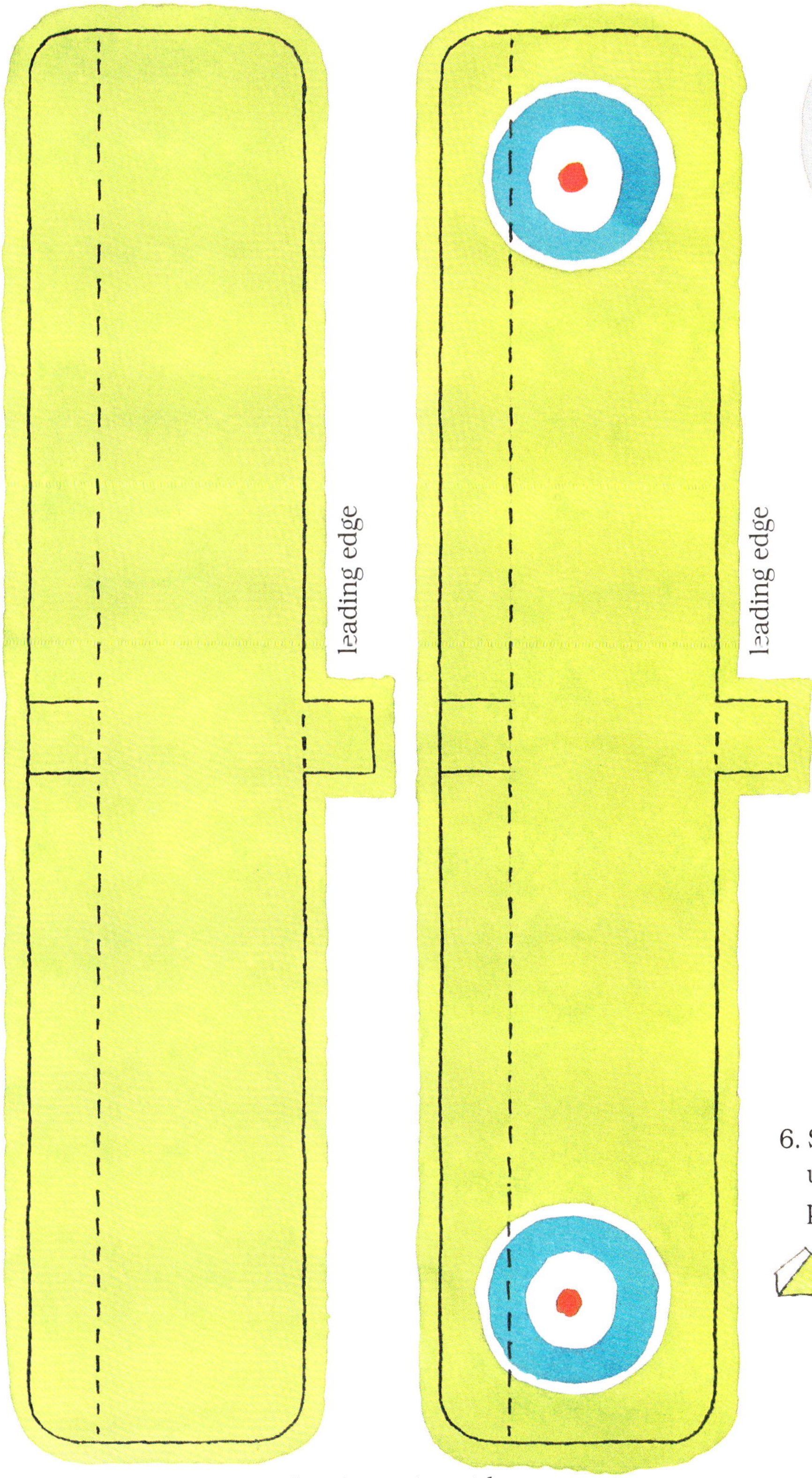


main wings—top side

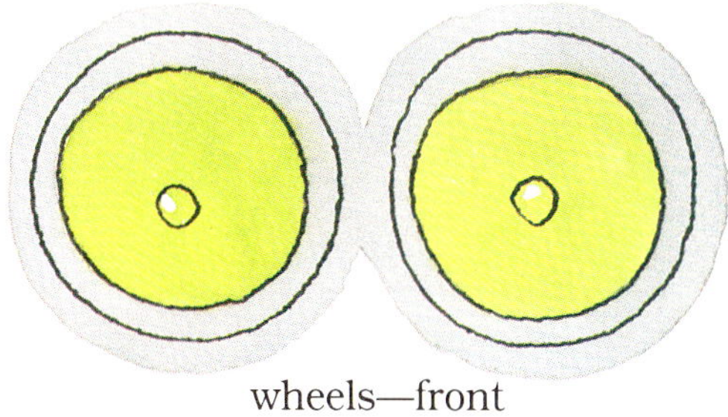

wheels—front

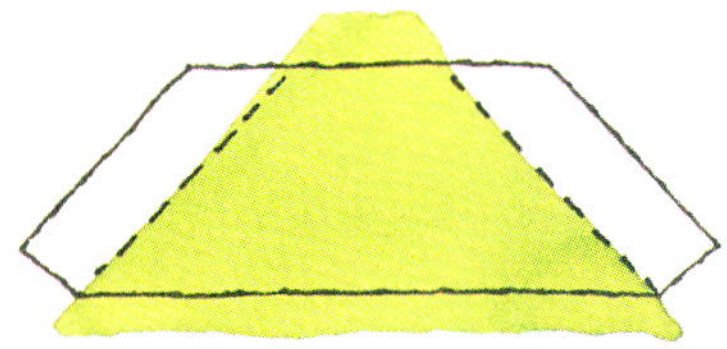

undercarriage—front

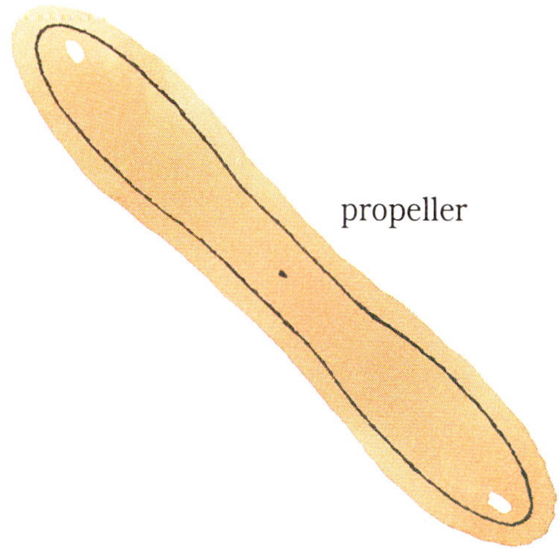

propeller

6. Score and fold the front of the undercarriage. Glue the undercarriage in place.

7. If desired for smoother landing, glue the wheels to buttons. Glue wheels onto the struts.

8. Attach the propeller.

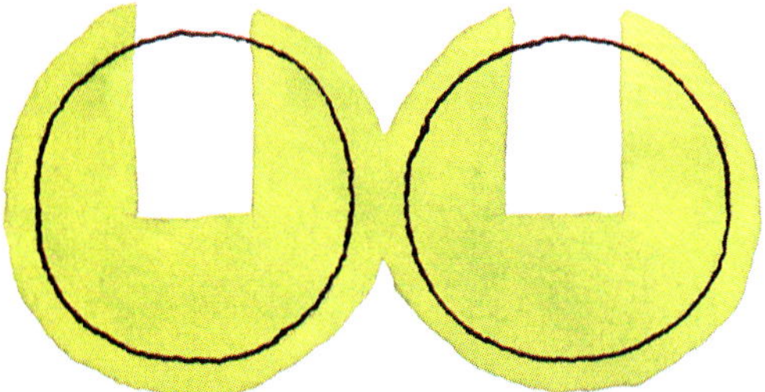

wheels—back

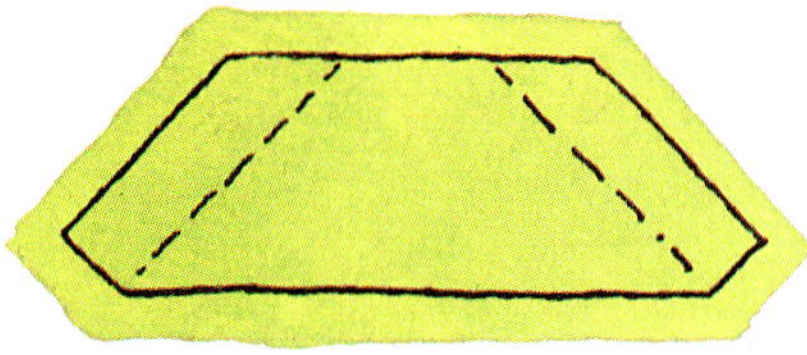

undercarriage—back

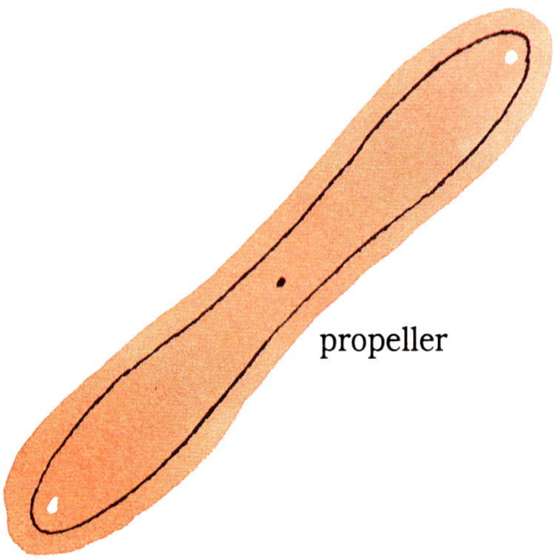

propeller

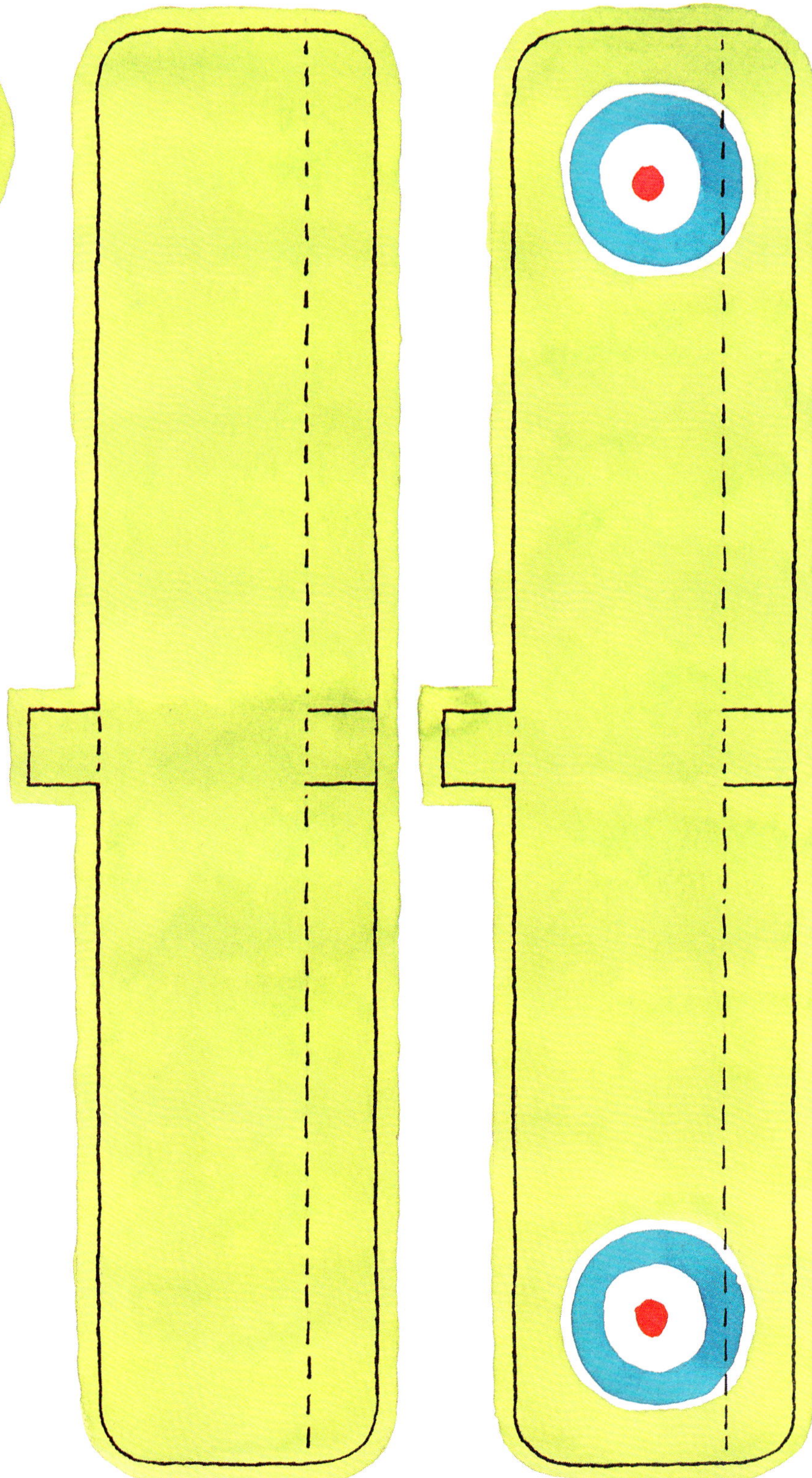

main wings—underside

A completed Sopwith Camel

Cut along this dotted line to remove page.

# The Supermarine Spitfire and the Messerschmitt 109

These were two famous fighter planes from World War II.

## The Supermarine Spitfire

Englishman R.J. Mitchell was an expert designer of racing sea planes. His streamlined Supermarine aircraft won the Schneider Cup in European speed trials four times.

In 1931, one of Mitchell's sea planes broke the world speed record when it flew at over 400 m.p.h.

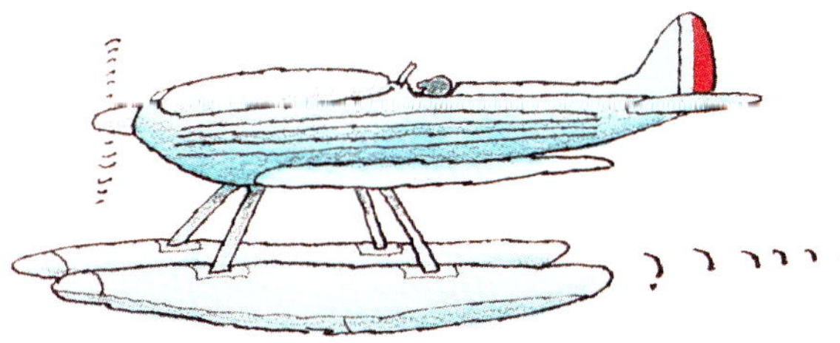

Mitchell's success in designing fast planes led the British government to ask him to design a fighter plane which could sustain a speed of 250 m.p.h. Mitchell knew that he could do even better—and proved it with his Supermarine 300, first flown in March 1936, which had a top speed of 350 m.p.h. It was nicknamed the Spitfire and became an important part of aviation history in World War II.

## The Messerschmitt 109

The Messerschmitt 109 was designed and built in 1935 by a team headed by Willy Messerschmitt, a famous German engineer who was best known for building light passenger aircraft. This was his first attempt at creating a fighter plane.

Many flying experts did not believe that Messerschmitt's new design would work. One flying ace, Ernst Udet, scoffed, "That little thing will never make a fighter." Udet was wrong. The Messerschmitt was a strong, fast plane (354 m.p.h.), and it became one of the most successful fighter planes of all time. More than 30,000 of these planes were built between 1937 and 1944.

The Messerschmitt 109 was unveiled to the public at the Olympic Games in Berlin in 1936.

Cut along this dotted line to remove page.

# Messerschmitt 109 model

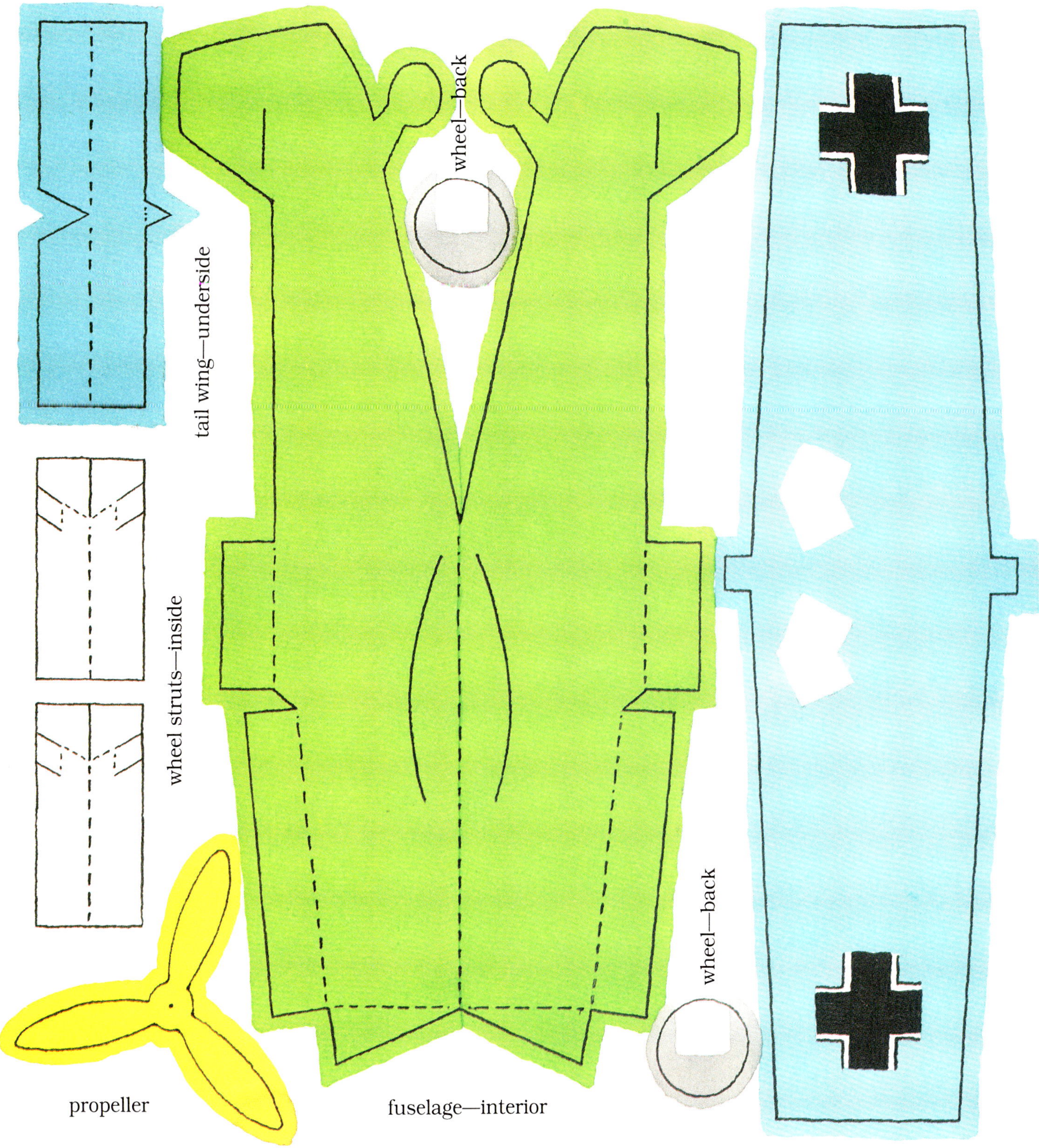


Cut along the solid lines.
Fold along the dotted lines.

# Messerschmitt 109—assembly

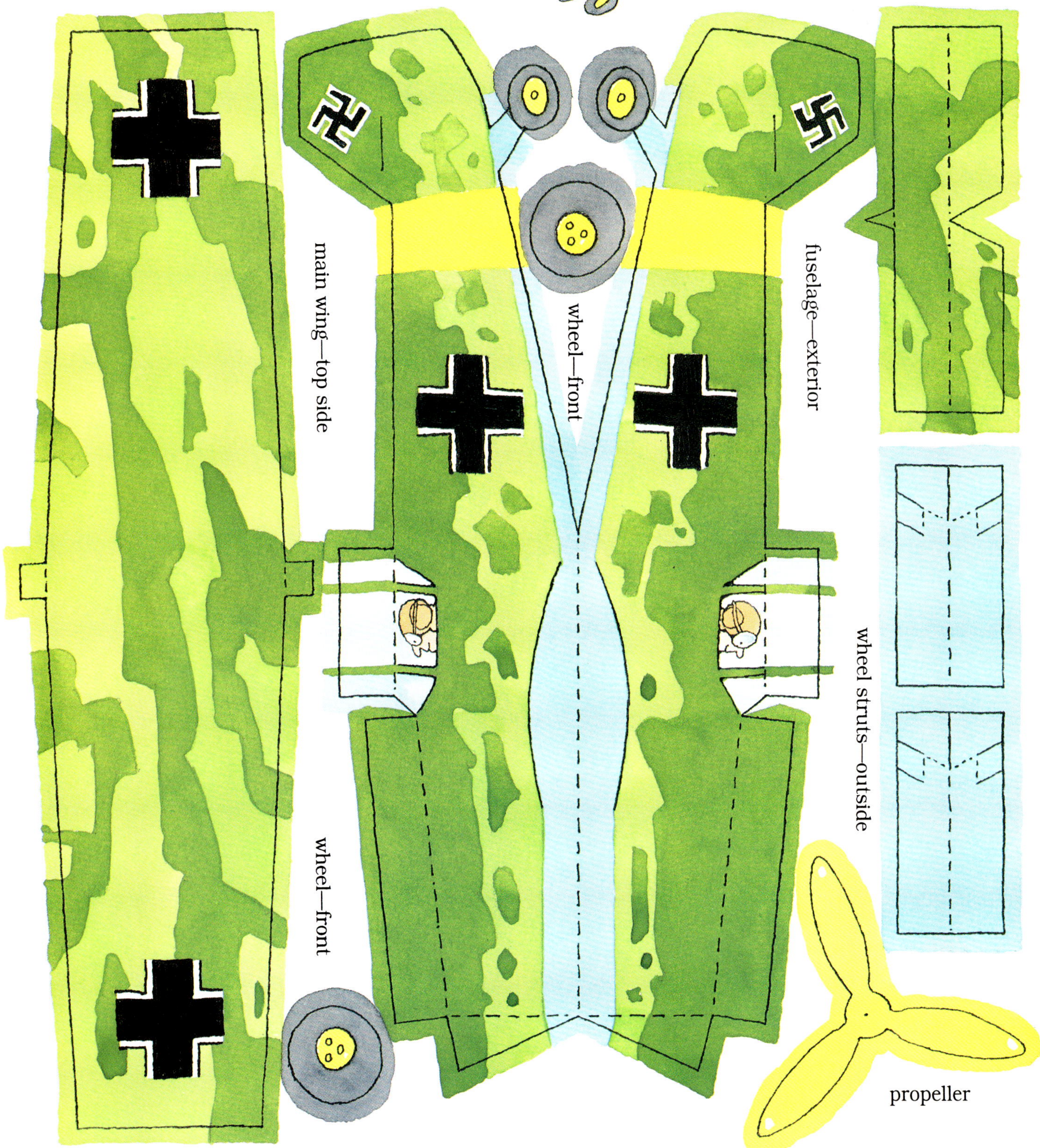


Cut along this dotted line to remove page.

1. Score and fold the fuselage.

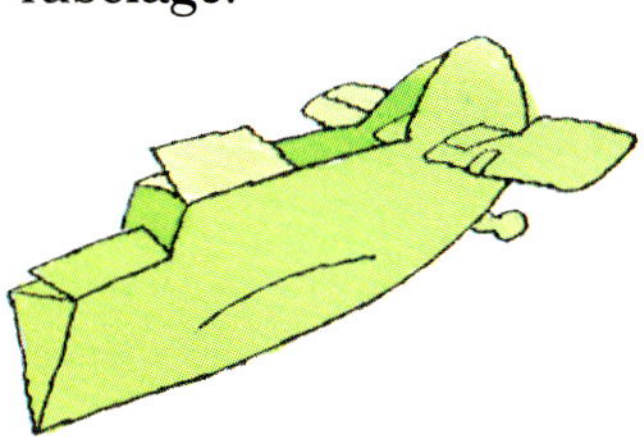

2. Cut slot and insert the tail wing.

3. Cut slots and insert the main wings.

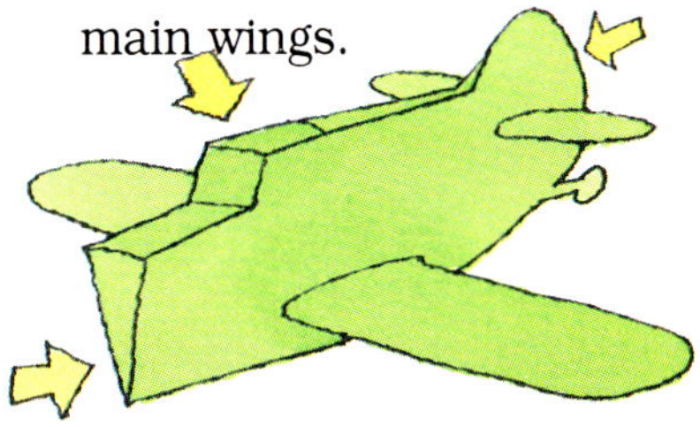

Cut along this dotted line to remove page.

# Supermarine Spitfire  model

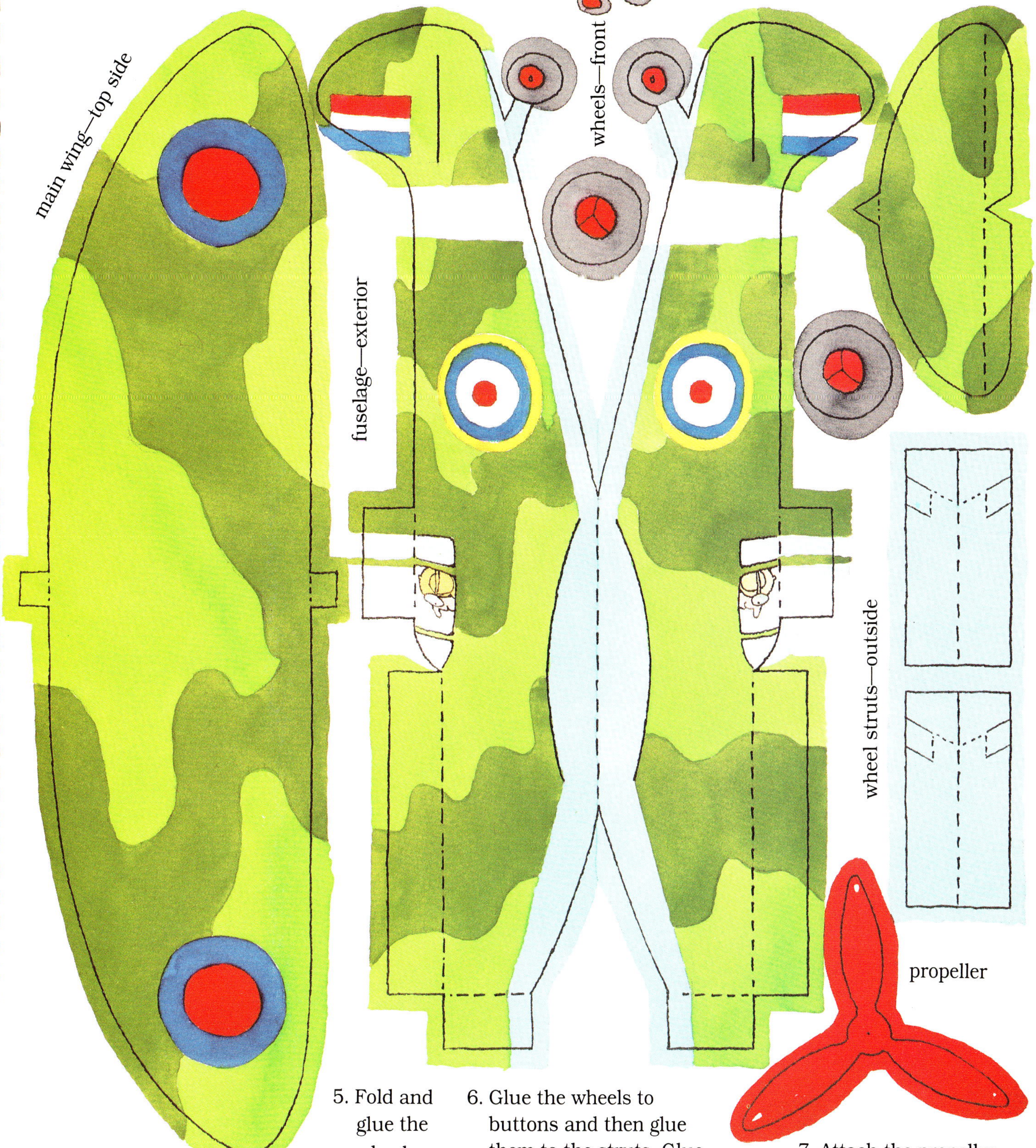


5. Fold and glue the wheel struts.

6. Glue the wheels to buttons and then glue them to the struts. Glue the struts under the wings.

7. Attach the propeller.

4. Glue the tail to the fuselage.

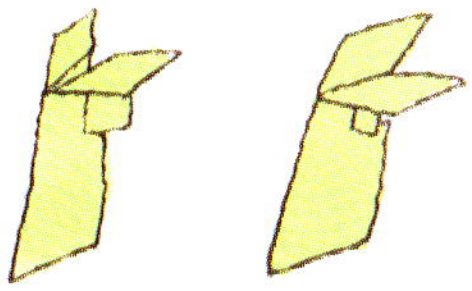

Cut along this dotted line to remove page.

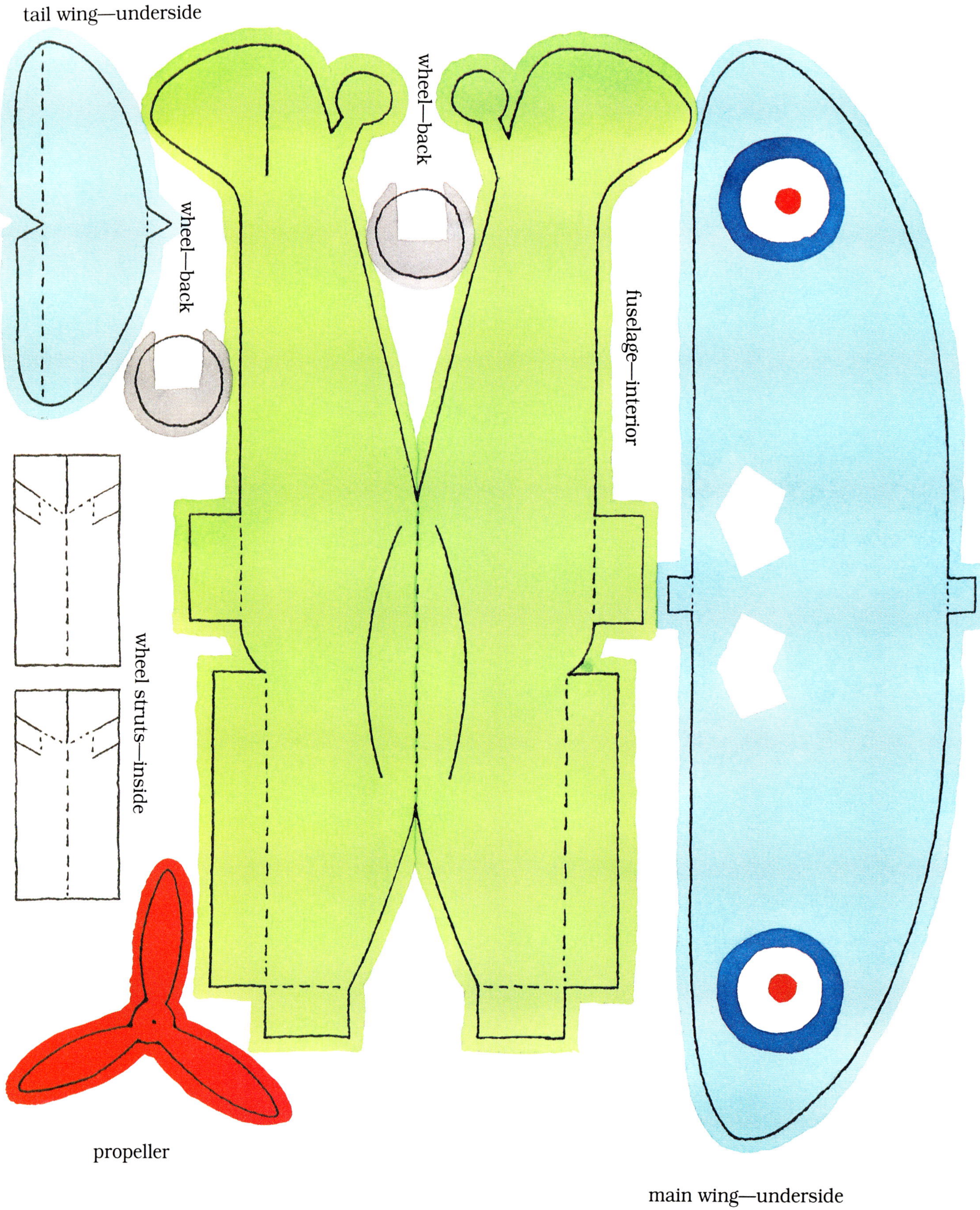

# The Development of Jets

The Gloster Meteor Mark I

In 1944, near the end of World War II, jet-powered fighter planes were used for the first time. Beginning in the mid-1930s, both British and German aeronautical engineers worked independently and secretly to develop jet-propelled aircraft engines, but jet planes did not become a reality until the middle of the war. The first two jets to see action were twin-engine fighters. Britain's Gloster Meteor Mark I was fast and reliable, flying at speeds of over 400 m.p.h. The Meteor was successfully used to defend Britain against flying bomb and rocket attacks.

Germany's Messerschmitt Me 262 jet fighter was even faster than the Meteor, flying at over 500 m.p.h., but was much harder to control. It was a dangerous craft in the hands of the great German flying aces of the Luftwaffe, but was introduced too late to have an impact on the outcome of the air war.

Messerschmitt Me 262

Once the war ended, the real work began on the next great development in aviation history—the commercial jet airliner.

The first commercial jet airliner, the British Comet, was built by the de Havilland Company. The original design, the DH 108, was an unusual tailless jet with swept-back wings. Making its first flight in 1946, it was both fast and efficient. But it was a poor design for a passenger plane, and a new one, the DH 106 Comet 1, made its debut three years later. Fast and comfortable, it became the first jet airliner in commercial service when it carried 36 passengers from London to Johannesburg.

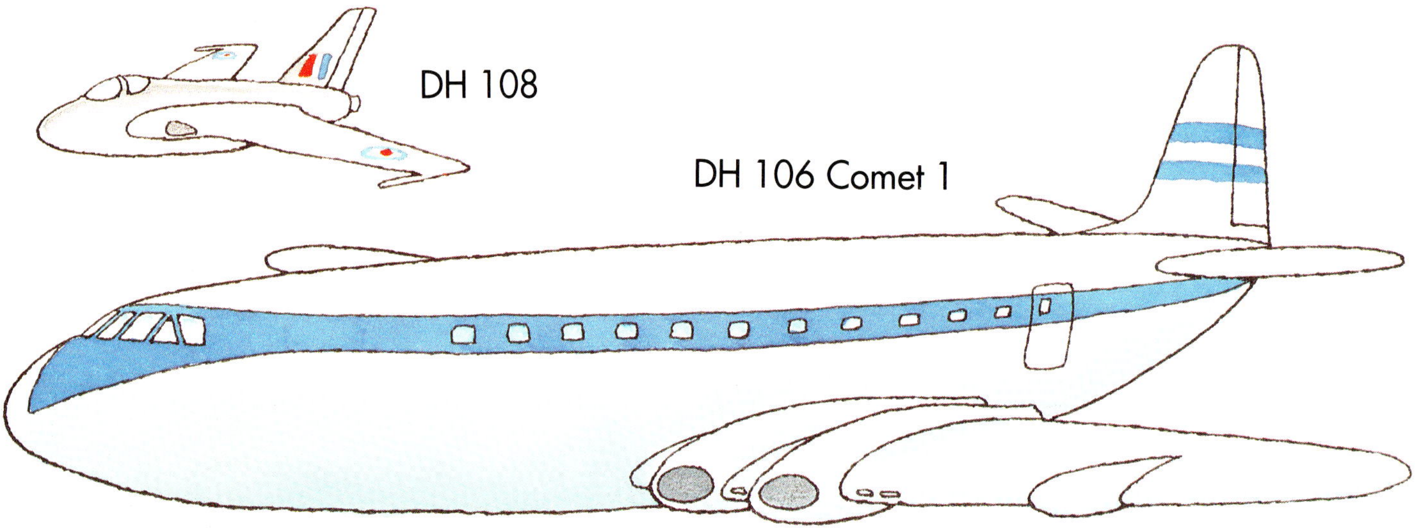


By 1954, the Boeing Company in the United States had designed an even more successful airliner, the Boeing 707. Worldwide air travel became possible for more and more people, and the demand for business and vacation flights grew. By the mid-1960s, Boeing began the development of the 747 Jumbo Jet, an airliner which would revolutionize commercial air travel. The 747 first flew in 1969, and, carrying up to 500 passengers, it remains one of the world's most popular aircraft.

# Supersonic flight

## The Concorde

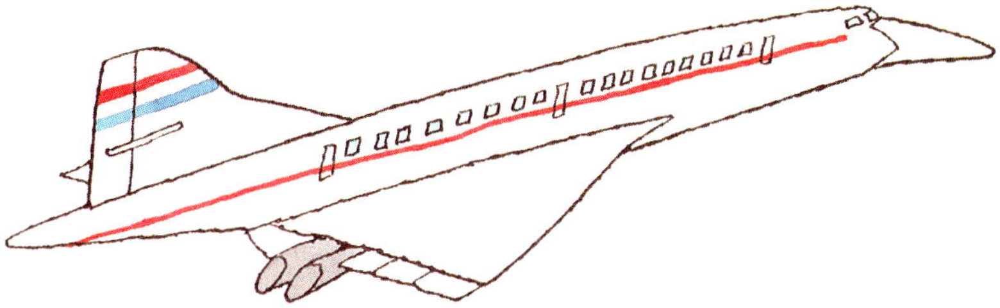

In 1962, the British Aircraft Corporation and the French *Aérospatiale* joined forces to develop the first supersonic airliner.

The world's costliest airliner made its first test flight in 1969; but it wasn't until January, 1976, after 14 years of hard work, that passenger service began. The Air France Concorde flew from Paris to Rio de Janeiro, and the British Airways Concorde flew from London to Bahrain. Service to New York began in November of 1977.

1. Nose and visor up.

The Concorde features a droop nose which drops down during taxiing, take-off, and landing so that the pilot can see clearly ahead.

2. Visor down.

In flight, the droop nose goes back into place and a visor window slides up into place over the windshield, creating a streamlined shape for supersonic flight.

3. Nose and visor down.

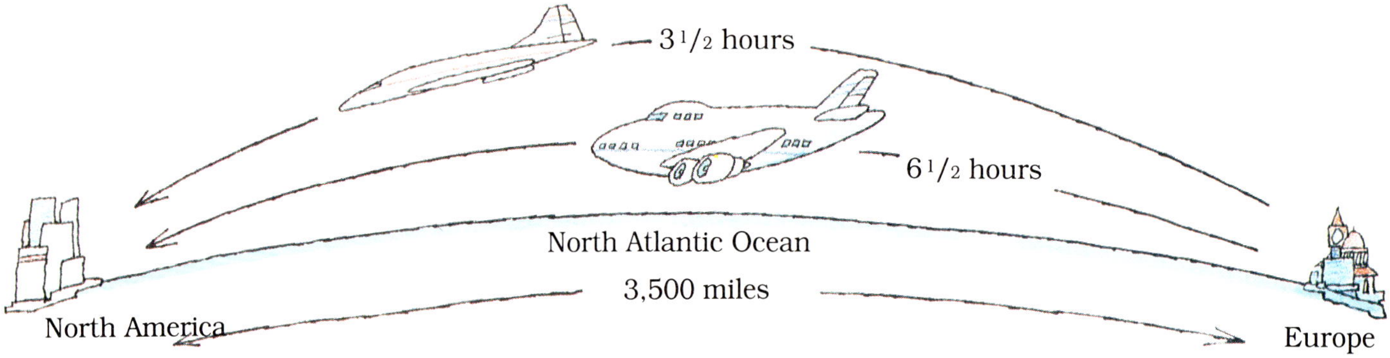


An ordinary airliner takes about 6 1/2 hours to fly across the North Atlantic; the Concorde makes the journey in less than 3 1/2 hours. The record Concorde flight from London to New York in 1980 took 2 hours, 59 minutes, and 14 seconds!

Traveling at supersonic speed means traveling faster than the speed of sound. At sea level, sound travels at about 760 m.p.h., but it travels more slowly at higher altitudes. The Concorde cruises at heights between 50,000 and 60,000 feet where the speed of sound is about 650 m.p.h.

The speed of sound is called Mach 1. The Concorde travels at Mach 2.2, more than twice the speed of sound.

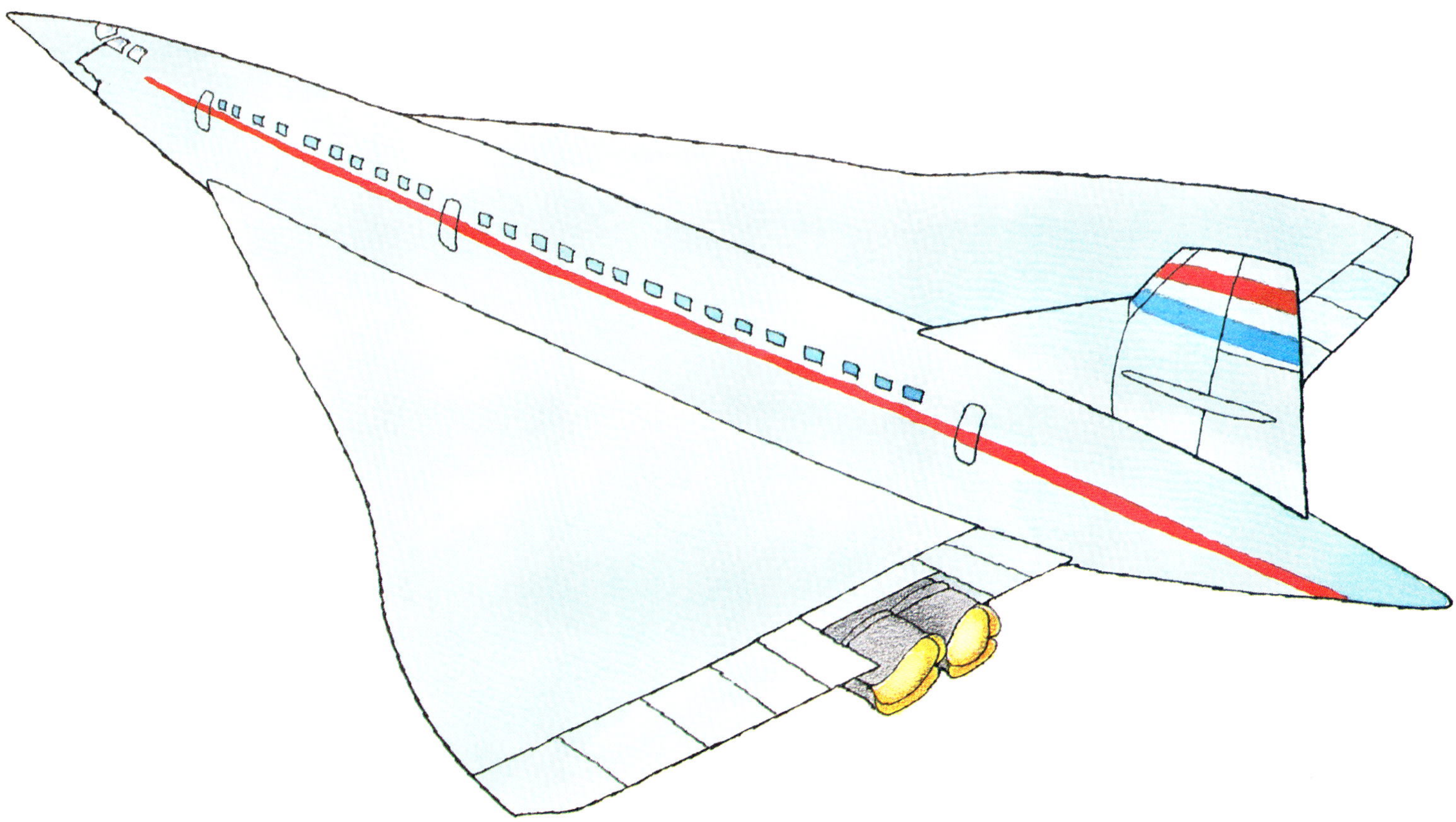

Cut along this dotted line to remove page.

# Concorde model

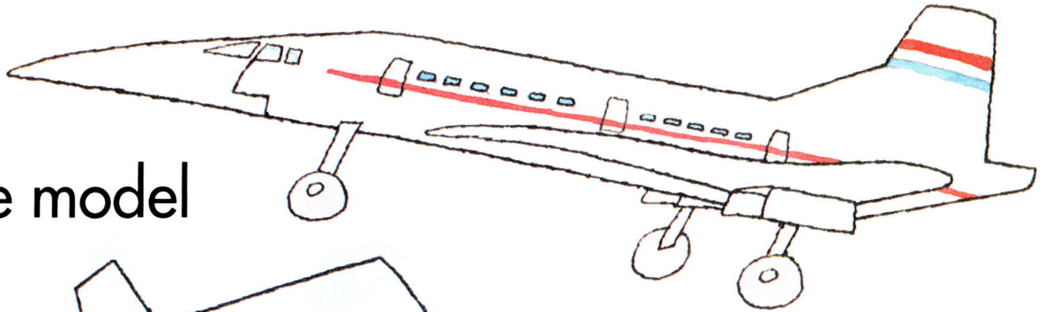

Cut along the solid lines.
Fold along the dotted lines.

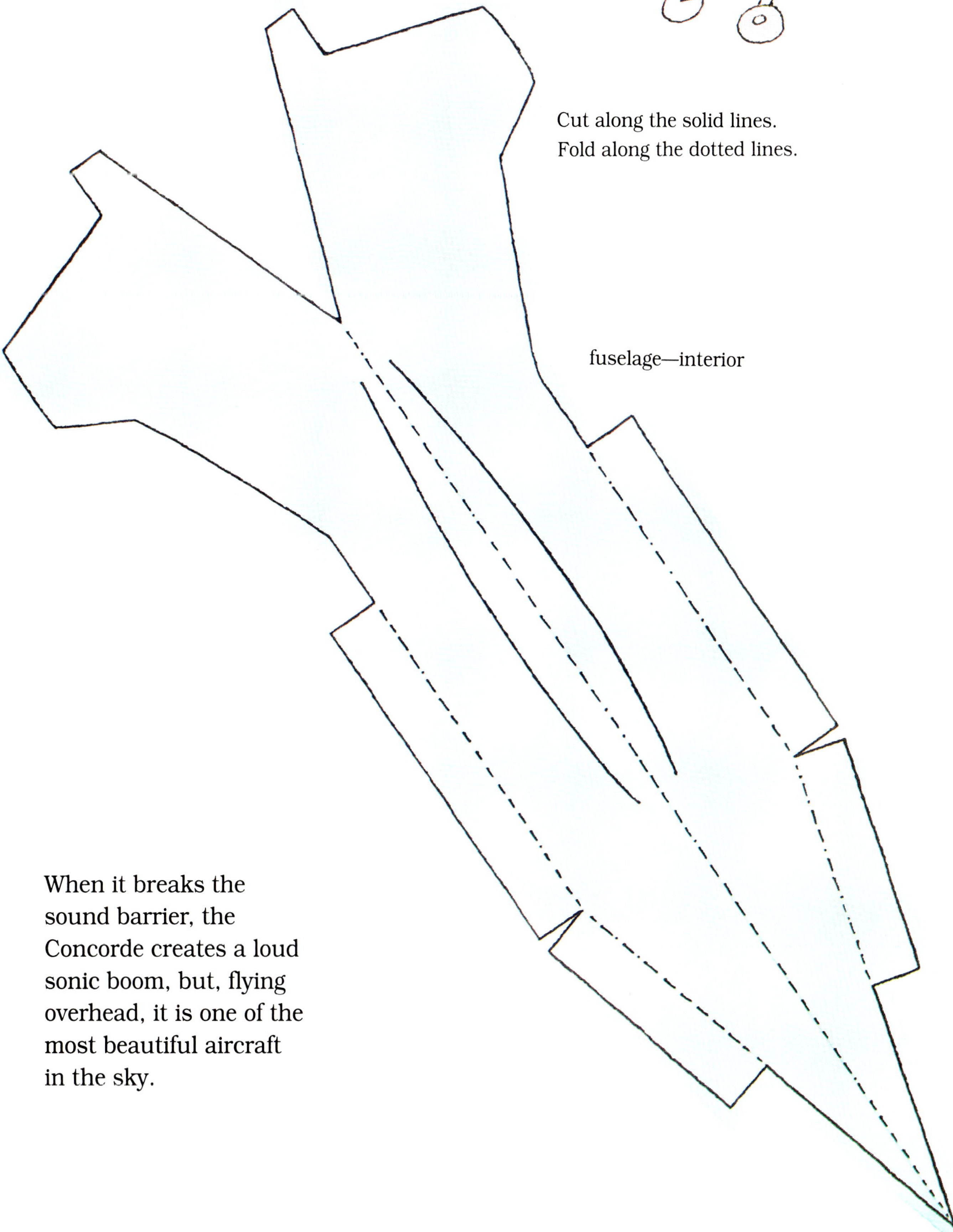


When it breaks the sound barrier, the Concorde creates a loud sonic boom, but, flying overhead, it is one of the most beautiful aircraft in the sky.

Concorde model—assembly

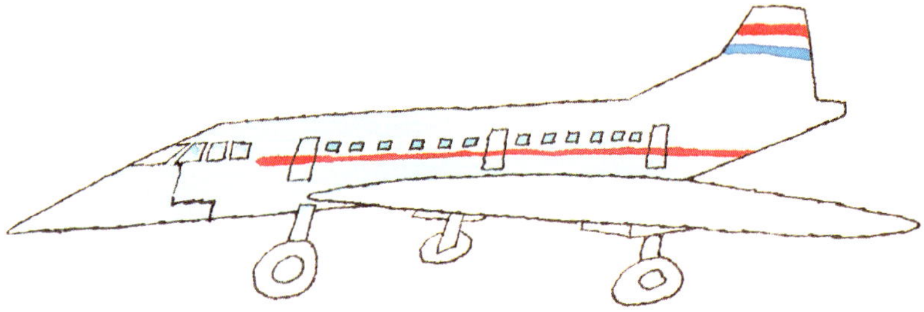

1. Score and fold the fuselage.

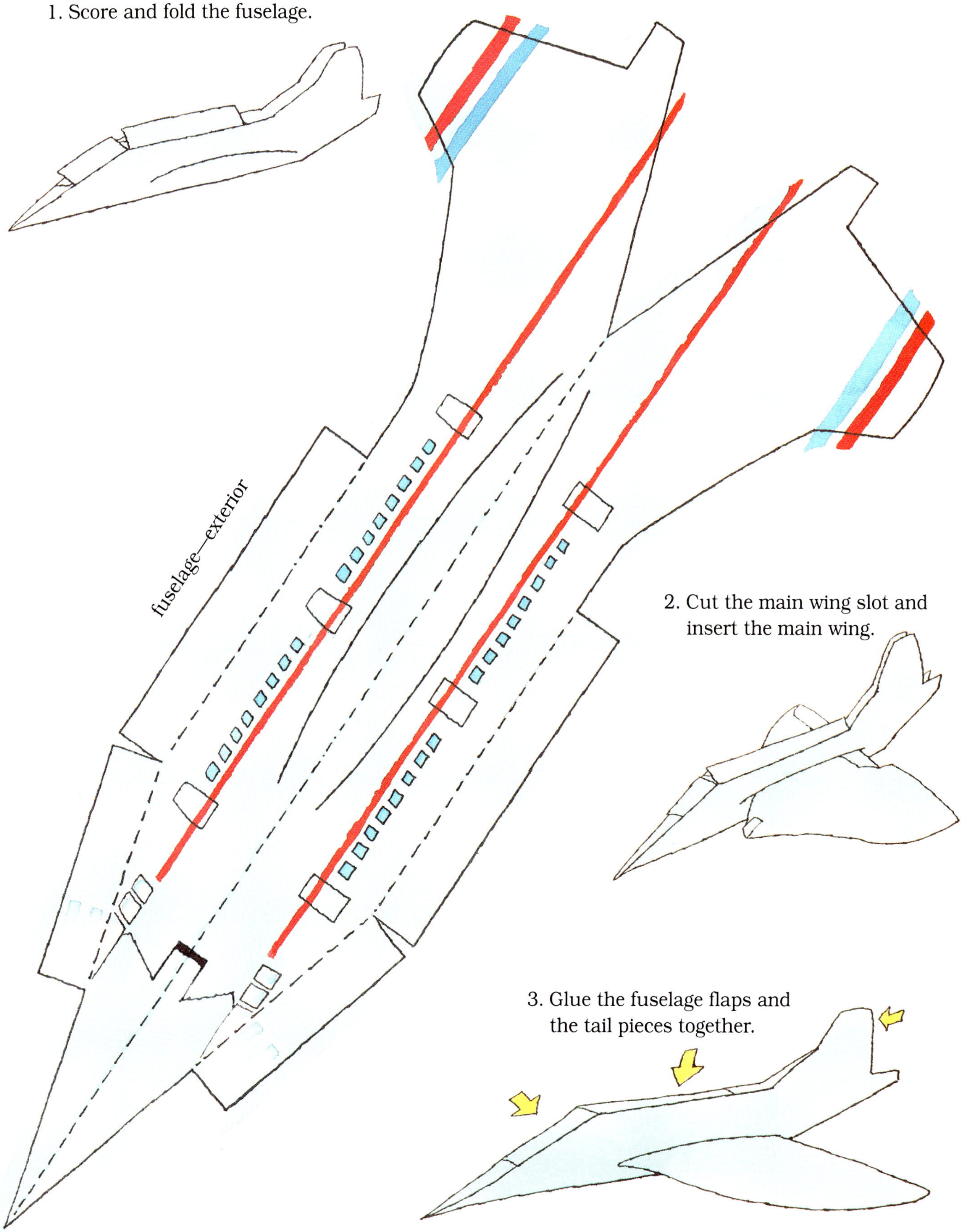


2. Cut the main wing slot and insert the main wing.

3. Glue the fuselage flaps and the tail pieces together.

Cut along this dotted line to remove page.

Cut along this dotted line to remove page.

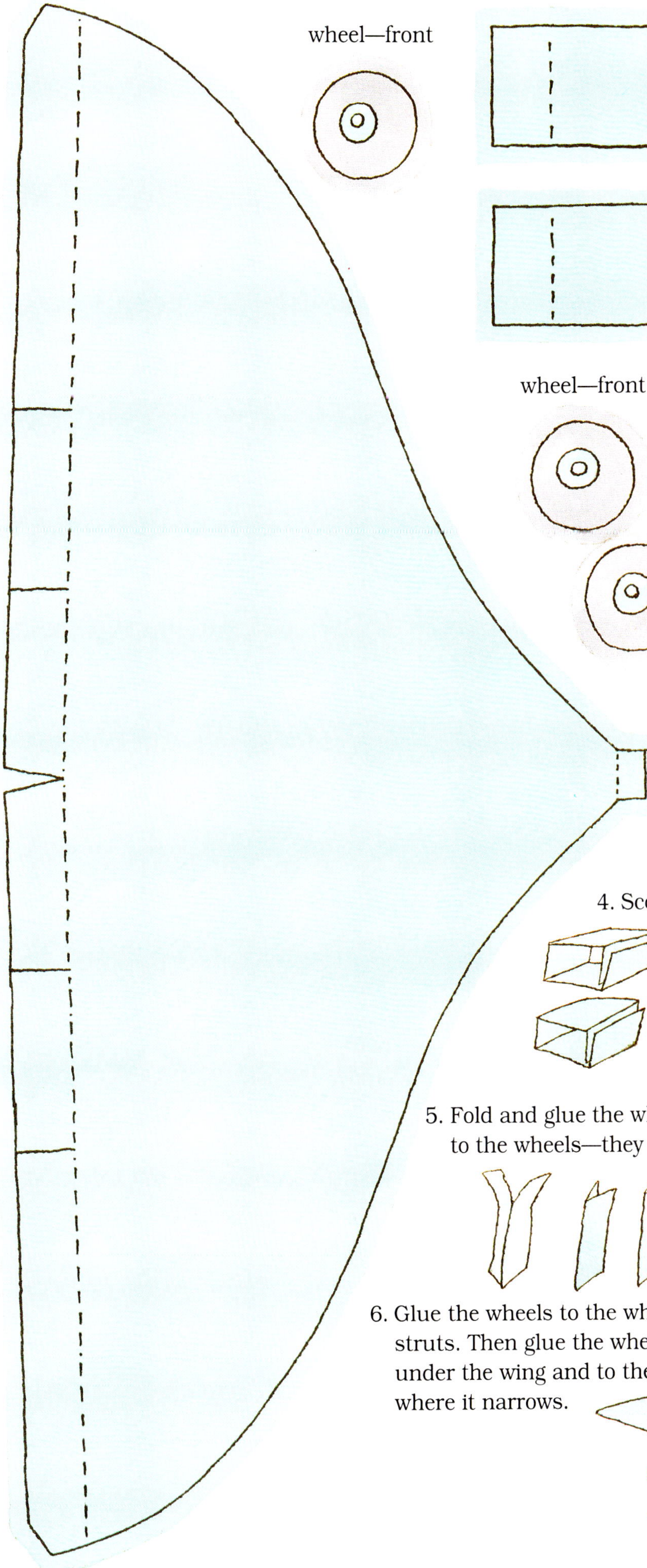

main wing—top side

wheel—front

engines

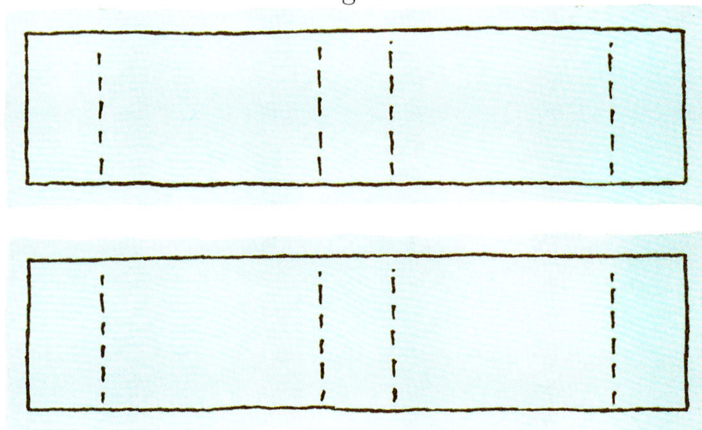

wheel—front

wheel struts—outside

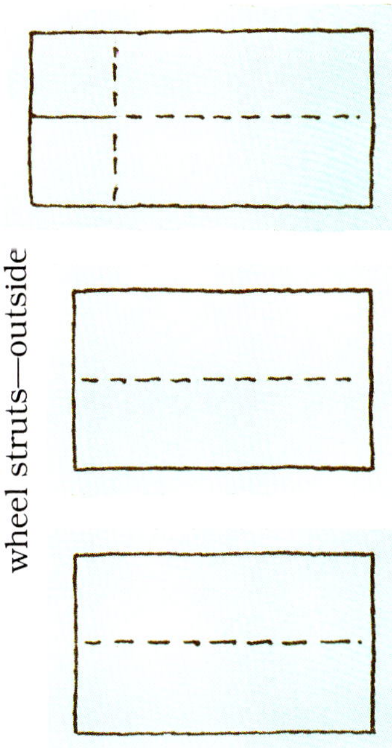

4. Score, fold, and glue the engines.

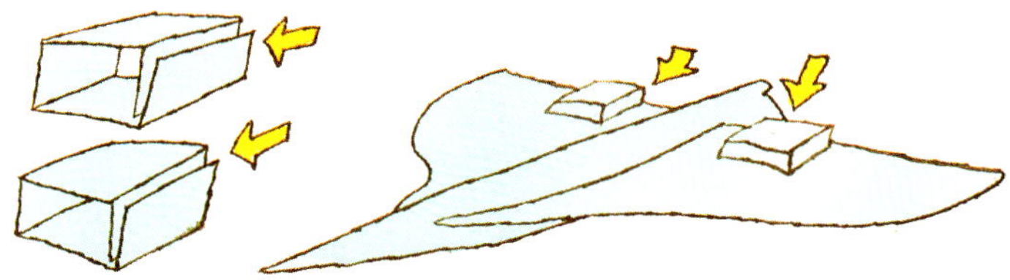

5. Fold and glue the wheel struts; allow to dry. If desired, glue buttons to the wheels—they add extra weight for smoother landings.

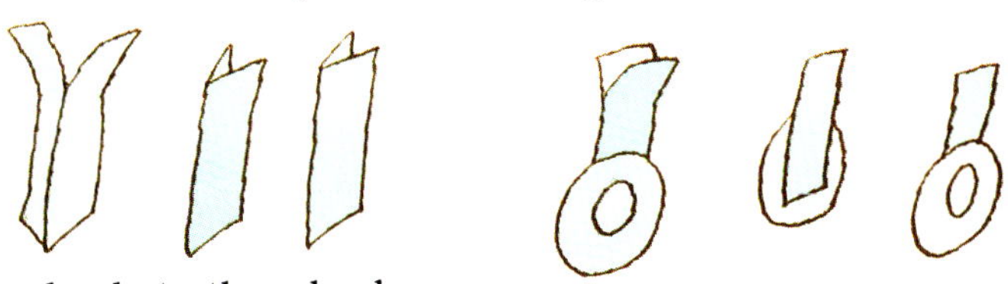

6. Glue the wheels to the wheel struts. Then glue the wheel struts under the wing and to the nose where it narrows.

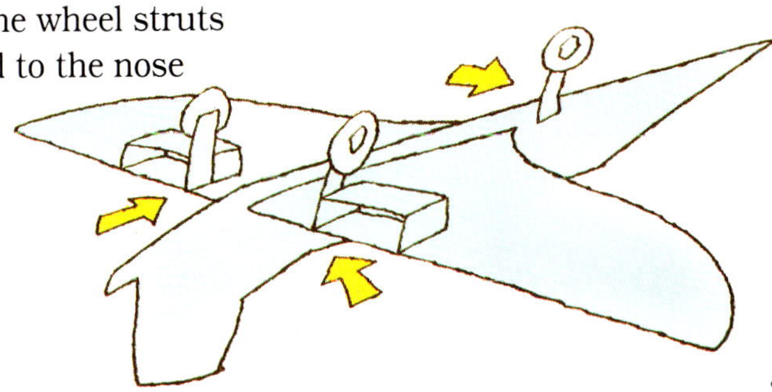

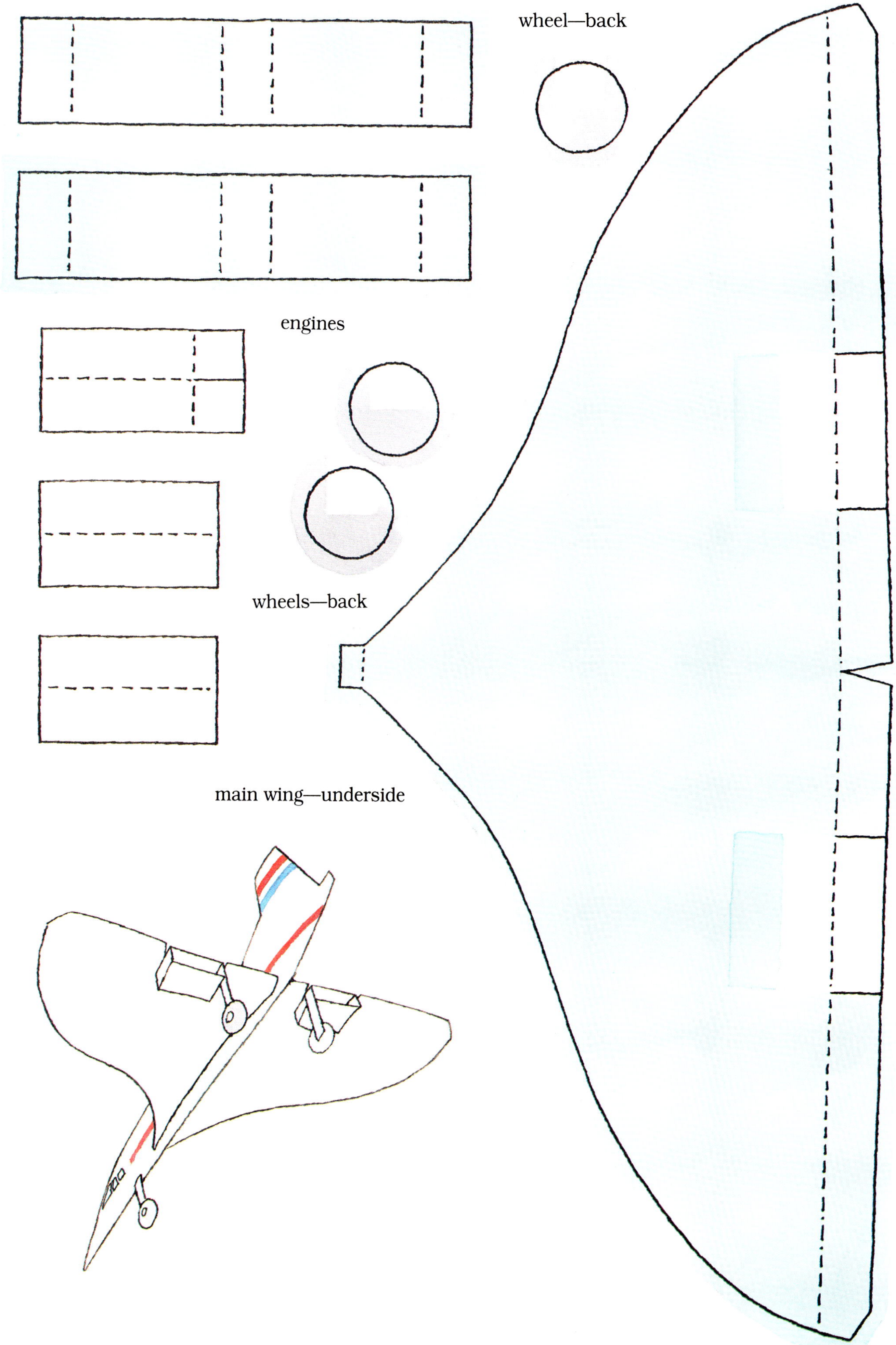


Cut along this dotted line to remove page.

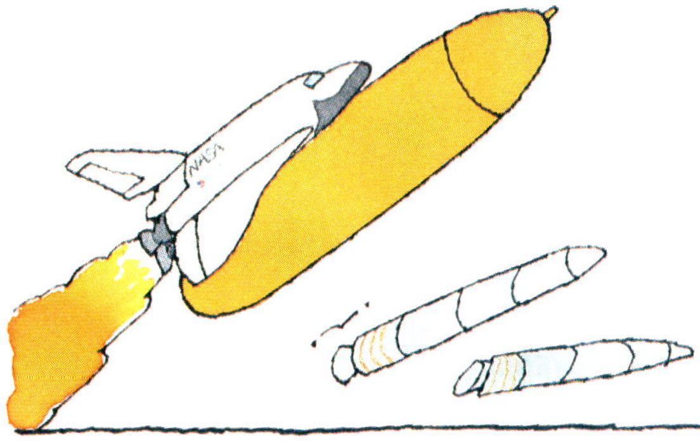

# The Space Shuttle

This spacecraft can go into space, return to Earth, land like an airplane, and be used again.

Traveling in space is very expensive and requires a large rocket with powerful engines and huge fuel tanks. Before the space shuttle, spacecraft engines were jettisoned as soon as the spacecraft had left Earth's atmosphere. The engines crashed into the sea and weren't used again. Even the orbiters—in which the first astronauts made their historic journeys—were unusable after their reentry into the atmosphere. These expensive craft could never bring cargo back to Earth or make a second journey.

In 1972, NASA (National Aeronautics and Space Administration) decided to build a spacecraft which could be used again and again. They spent ten billion dollars over the next ten years to create the space shuttle.

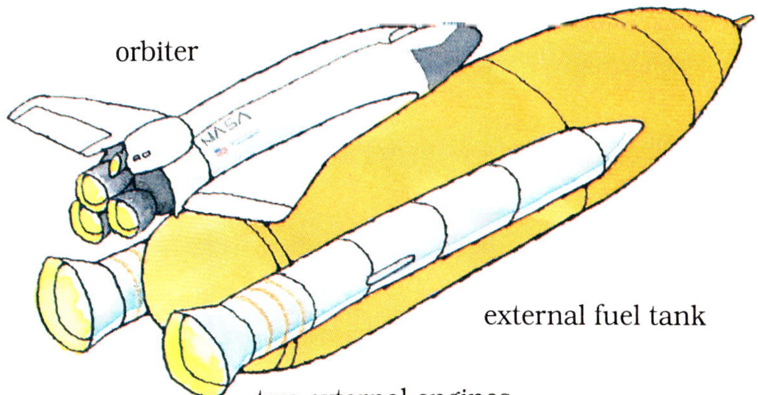


The orbiter is designed to take off like a rocket and land like a plane. The shuttle takes off with the orbiter's main engines boosted by two external engines. When they burn out, they are parachuted into the sea, where they are retrieved. At the edge of the atmosphere, the external fuel tank is jettisoned. It breaks up, and the pieces fall into the ocean.

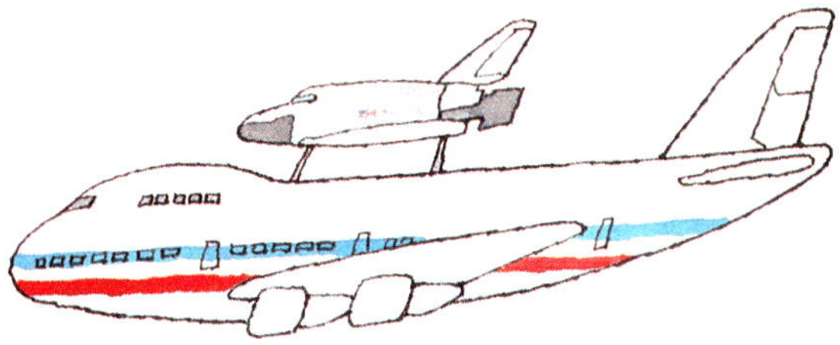

Built to determine the best method for shuttle landings, the test orbiter *Enterprise* was launched from a Boeing 747 Jumbo Jet.

On April 12, 1981, the *Columbia* became the first shuttle orbiter to fly in space and return safely. The successful two-day flight was commanded by John Young and piloted by Robert Crippen.

Shuttle orbiters have cargo bays which can be used for launching and repairing satellites, carrying laboratories, and launching spacecraft and telescopes in deep space.

Eventually, the space shuttle may even be used as a space truck to build a permanent, orbiting space station.

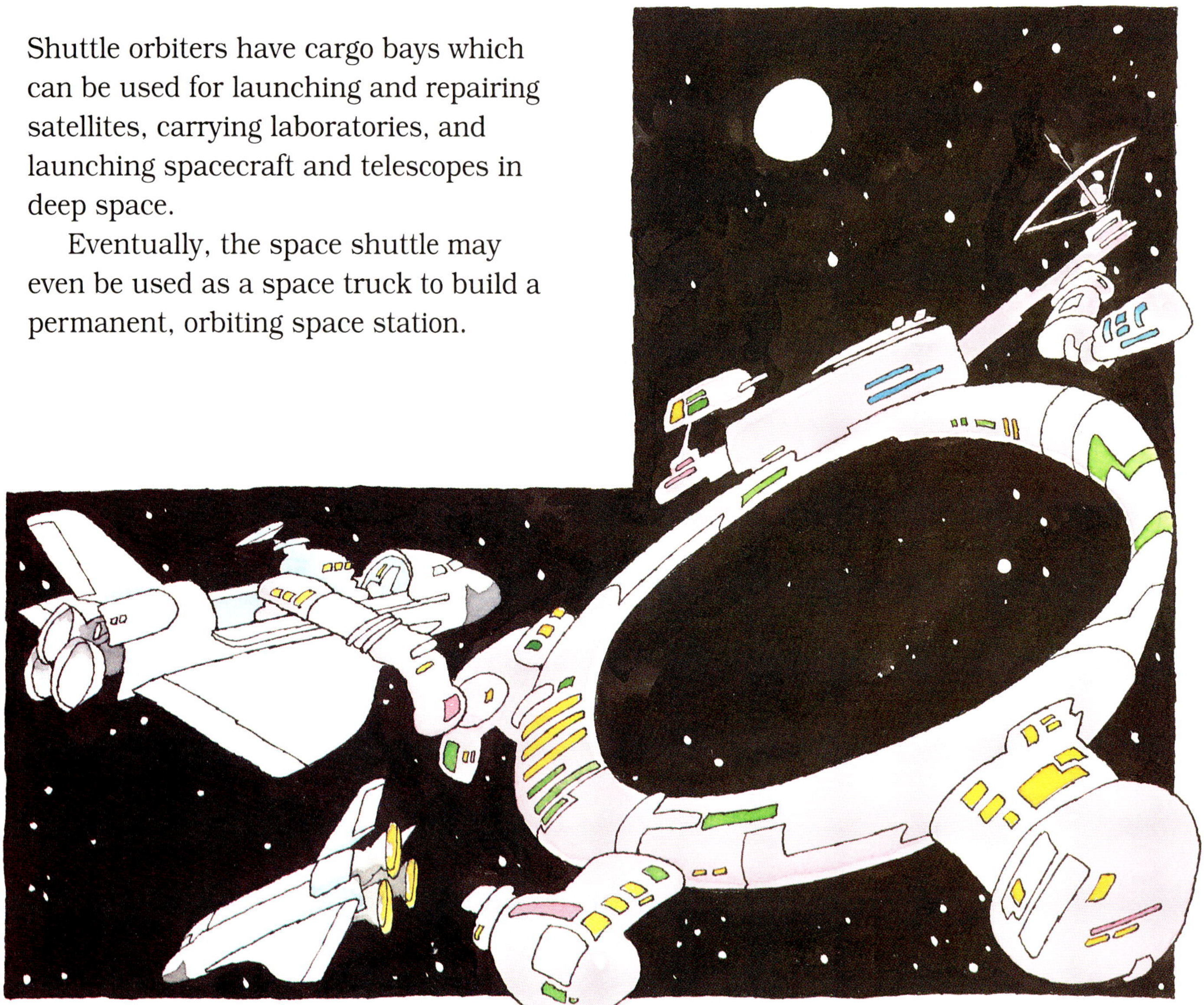

Cut along this dotted line to remove page.

# Space Shuttle model

Cut along the solid lines.
Fold along the dotted lines.

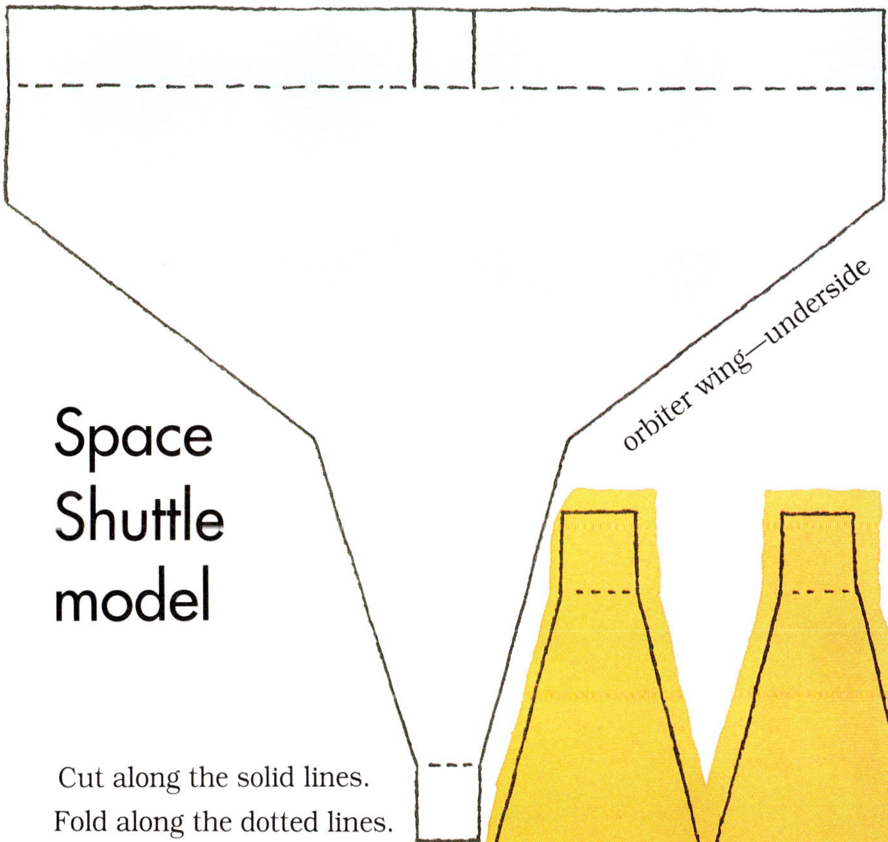


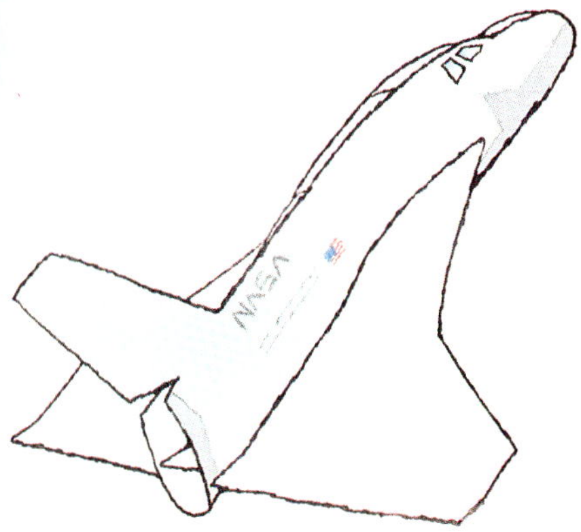

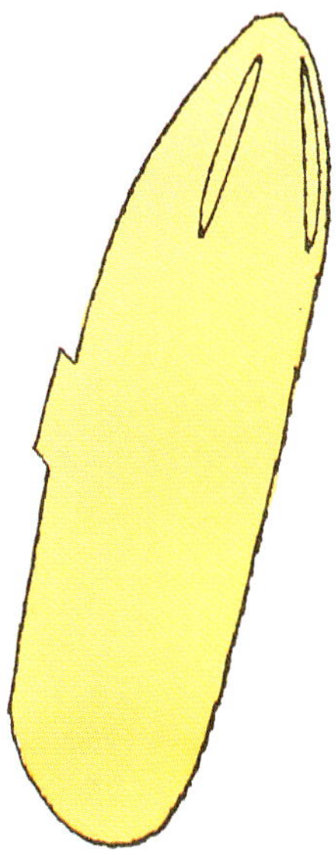

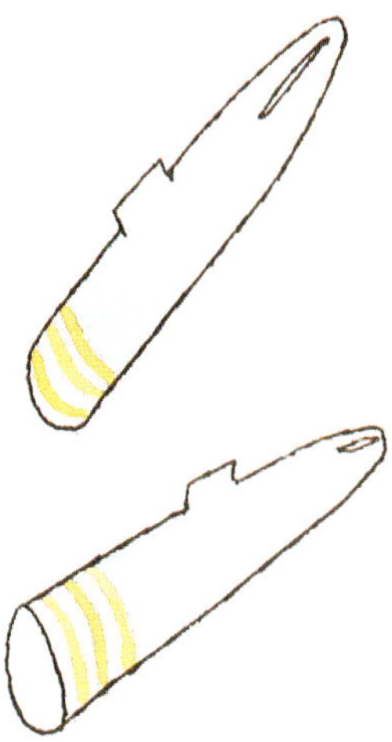

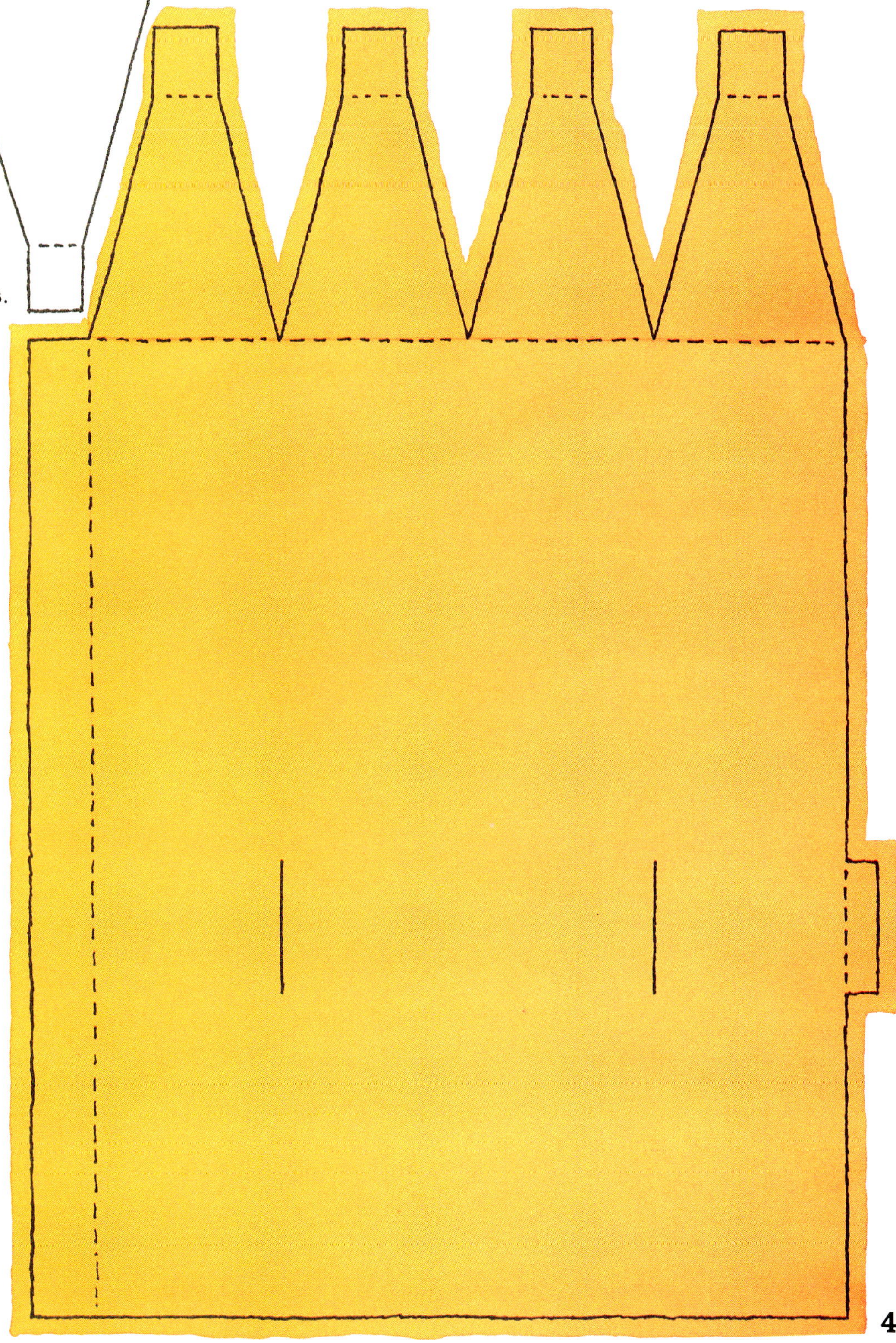

## Space Shuttle—assembly

Cut along the solid lines.
Fold along the dotted lines.

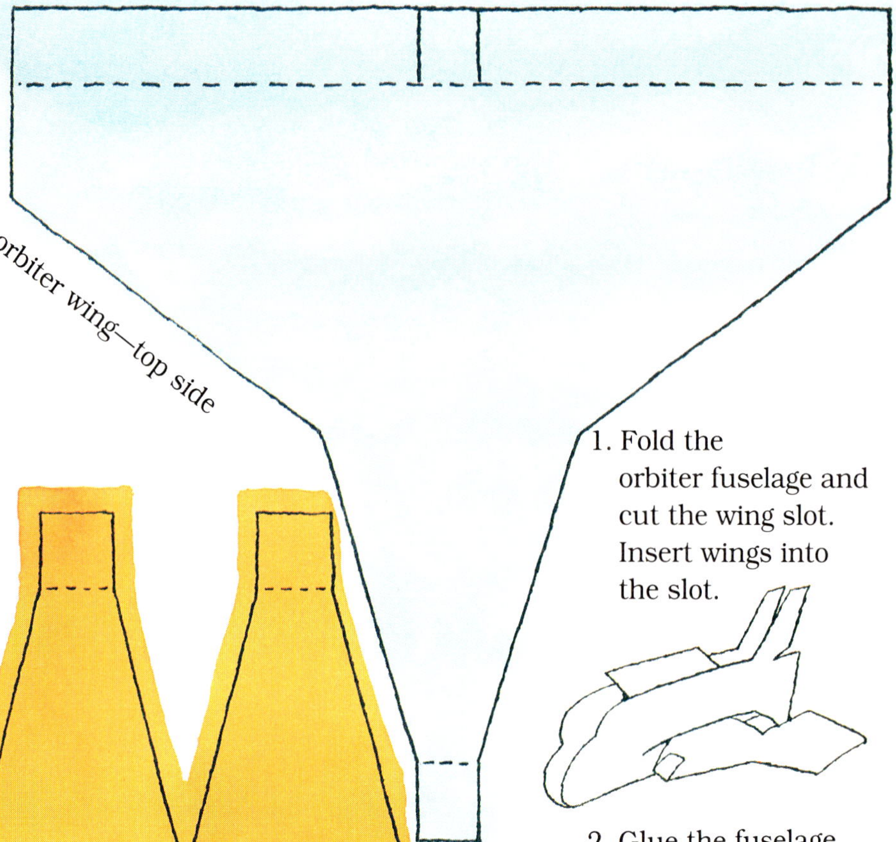


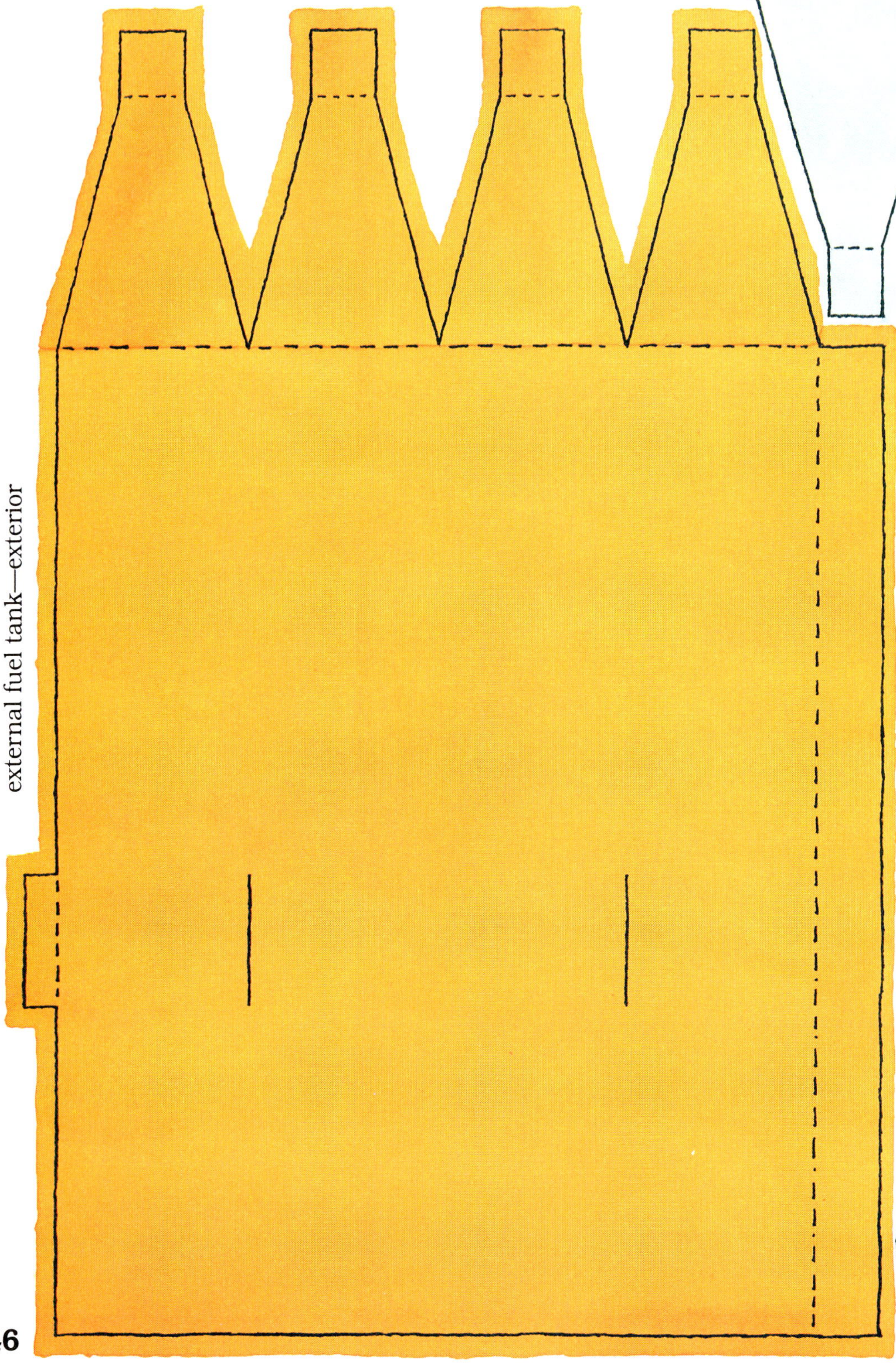


1. Fold the orbiter fuselage and cut the wing slot. Insert wings into the slot.

2. Glue the fuselage flaps and the tail.

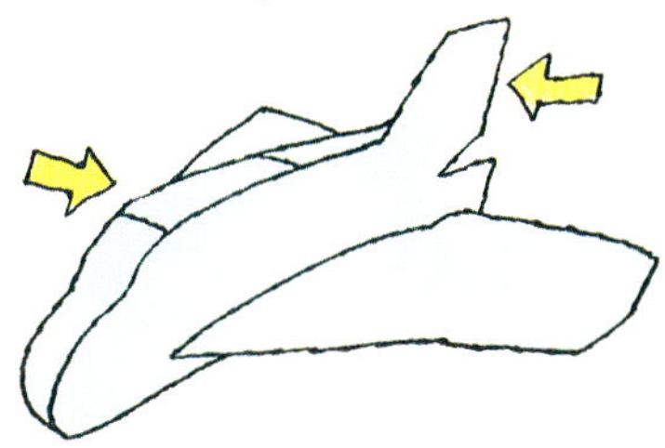

3. Fold and glue the external fuel tank.

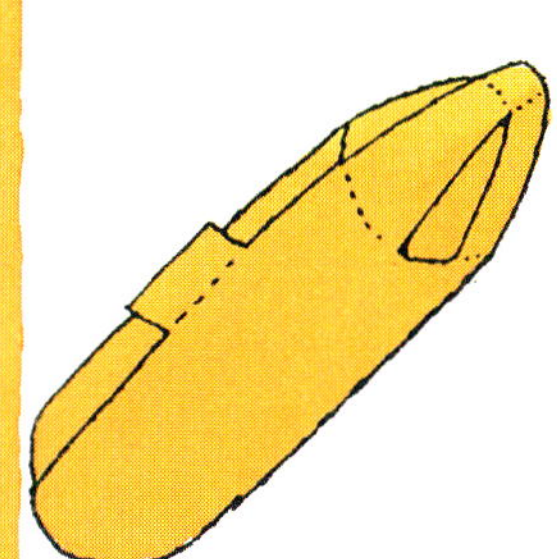

4. Fold and glue the external engines.

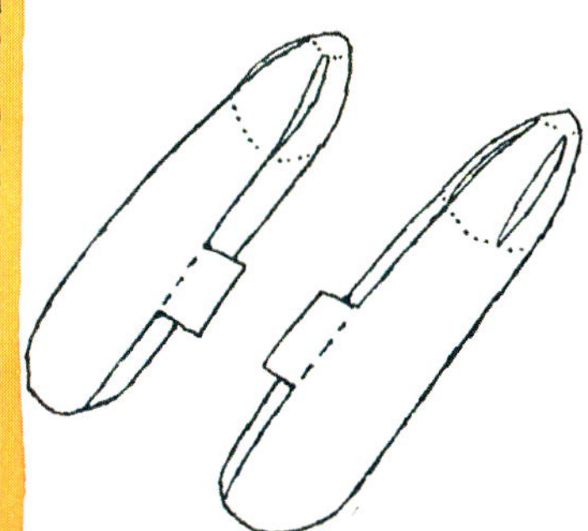

Cut along this dotted line to remove page.

Cut along this dotted line to remove page.

5. Slot orbiter and external fuel tank together.

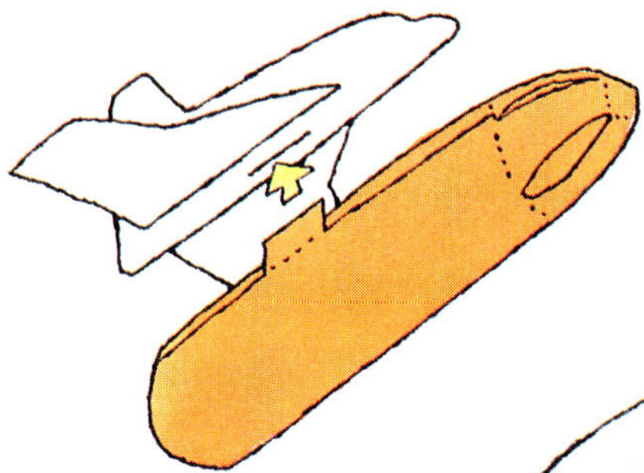

6. Slot the engines to the fuel tank.

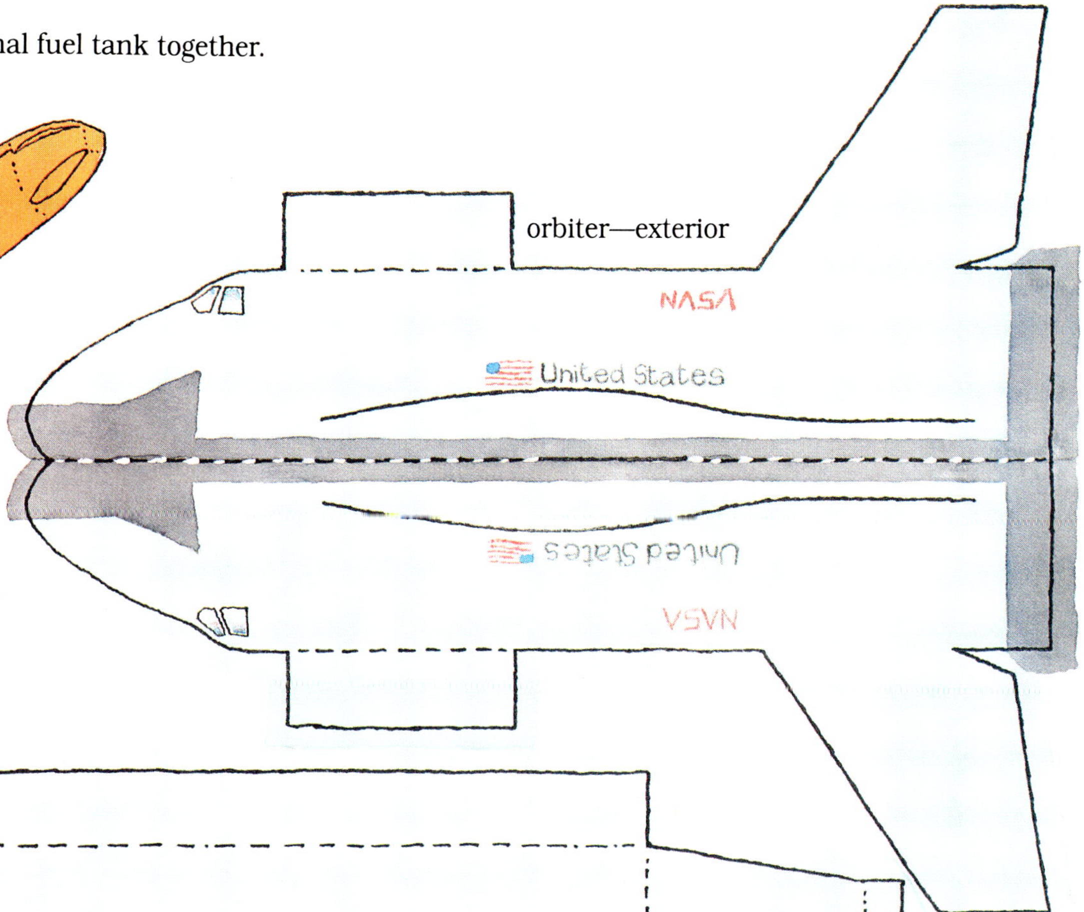


orbiter—exterior

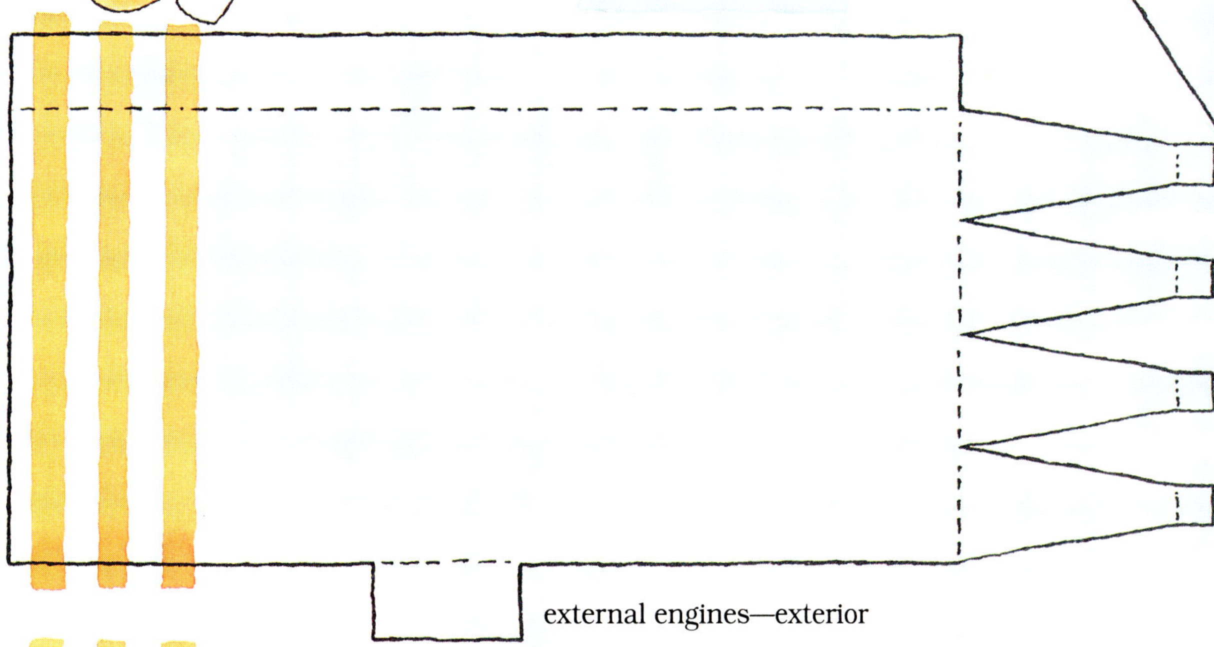

external engines—exterior

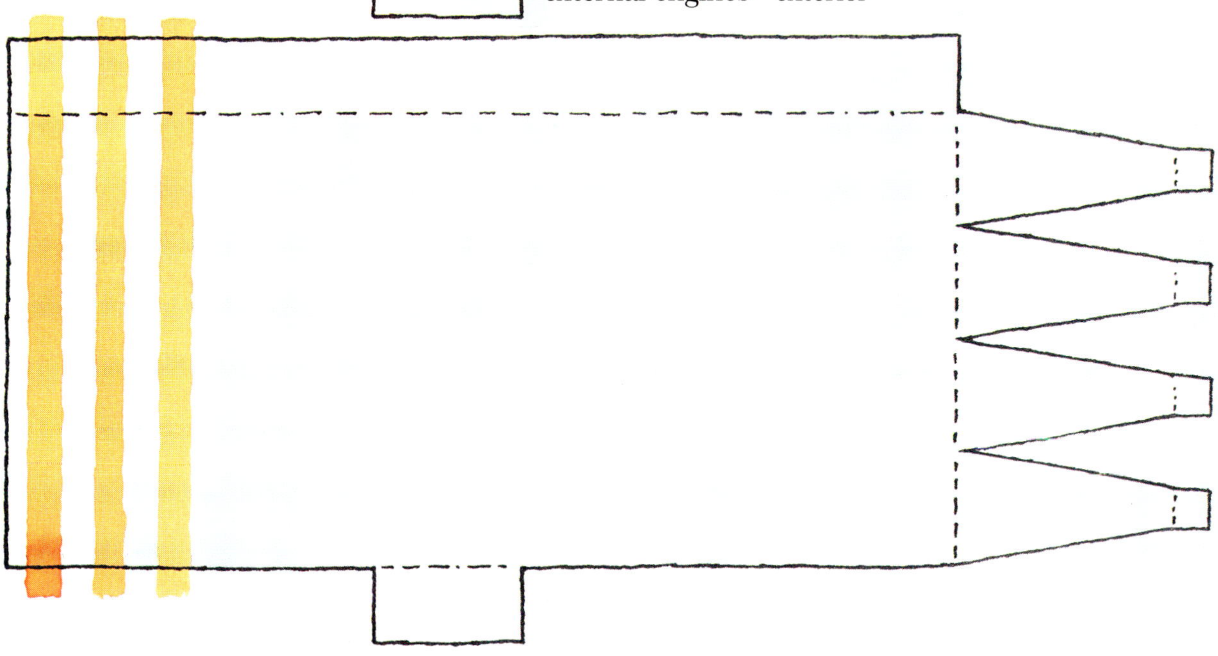

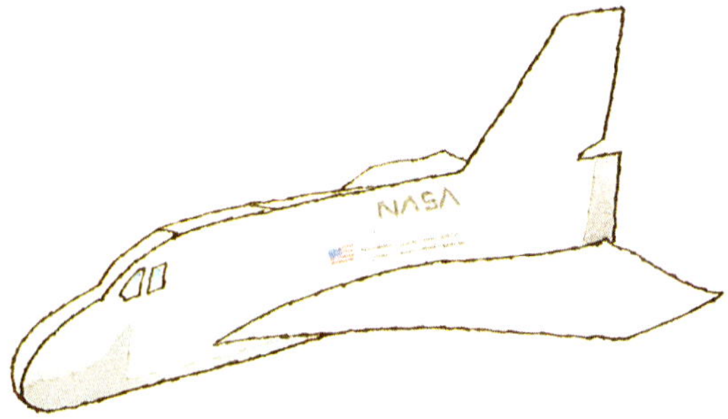


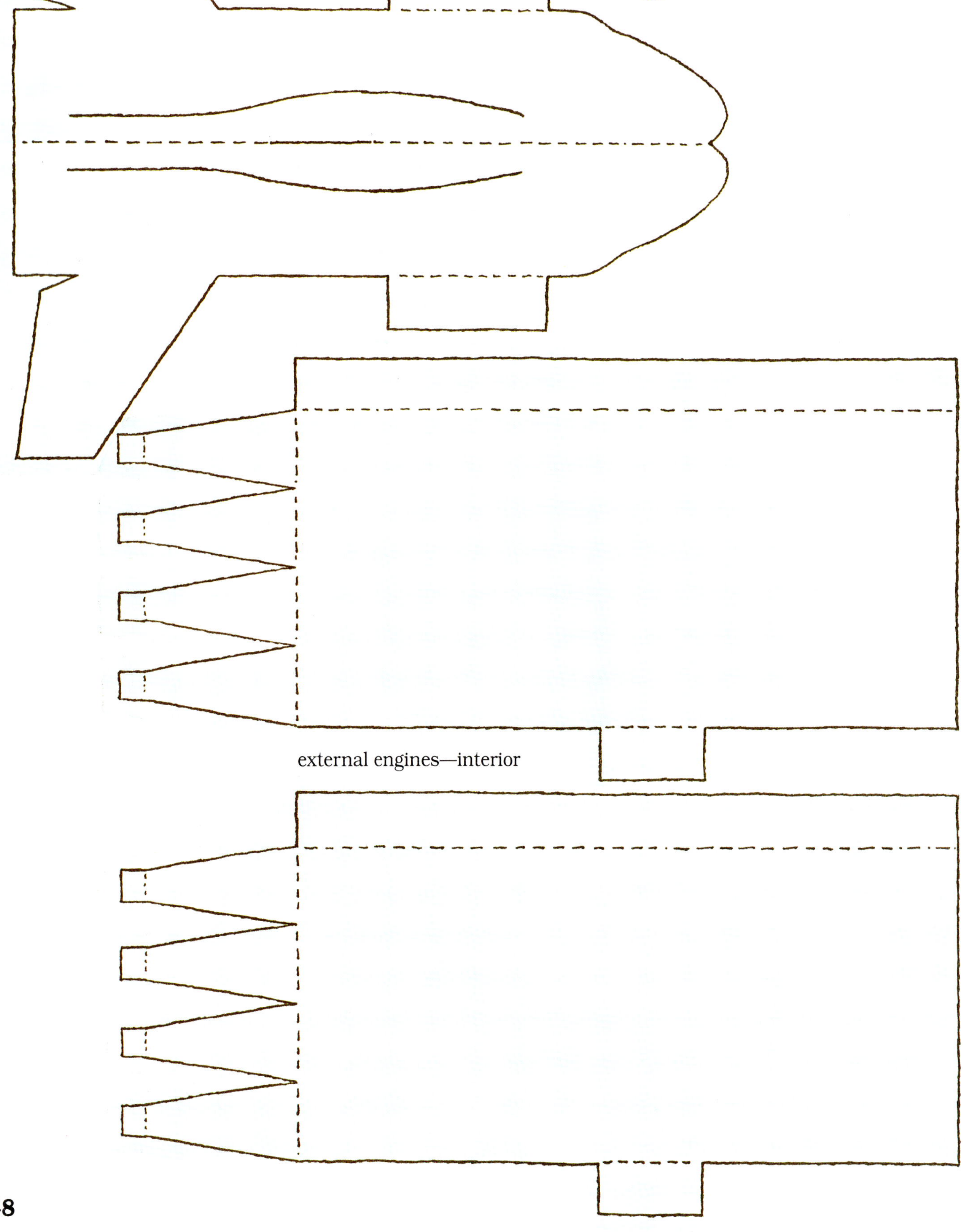


Cut along this dotted line to remove page.